Case History Of A Movie

Case History

of a Movie

BY DORE SCHARY

AS TOLD TO

CHARLES PALMER

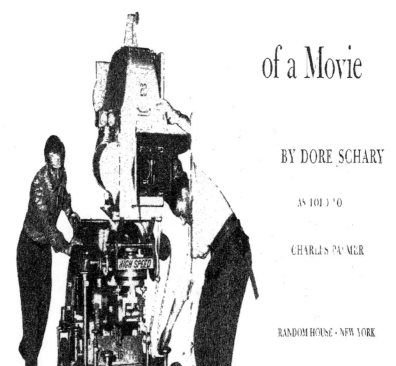

The grips move the camera
Head Grip Leo Morton at left

RANDOM HOUSE · NEW YORK

The author wishes to thank the New York *Times Magazine*
and *The Hollywood Reporter* for permission
to use material which appears in the final chapter of this book

Manufactured in the United States of America

Designer· Ernst Reichl

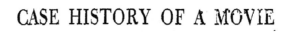

CASE HISTORY OF A MOVIE

FOR MIRIAM

GENERAL CONTENTS

CONTENTS

*position. Models and miniatures. Optical effects. The
lab.*

ILLUSTRATIONS

Nancy Davis awaits her fate at her audition reading. From left: Director Bill Wellman, Producer Dore Schary and co-star James Whitmore.

Pre-production cast rehearsal. Director Wellman indicates action for his stars on the set diagram.

The first scene on the schedule· Joe, young Johnny and Mary Smith at breakfast.

A painted scenic backing reproduces the location exterior as seen from Joe Smith's front door.

Assistant cameraman checks focus for a close shot.

Director Wellman gets in close to work out the shading of an intimate emotional scene.

The locker-room cast work out the scene while the set is being lighted.

Working out the action on a location exterior.

A typical stage crew at work.

Grips move a section of "wild wall" out of camera field.

Associate Art Director Eddie Imazu checks the model of the "Ext. Brannan Back Yard" set.

Electricians handle the lights, grips supply the shade. Head Grip Leo Monlon at far left; Gaffer Chet Philbrick in center.

Set Decorator Ralph Hurst seems to be in the wrong Prop Room for *The Next Voice*.

An actor's-eye view of the stage sound crew: Boom Man Fred Faust and Mixer Conrad Kahn.

"I cooked up something today. See what you think of it." Dore Schary, Eddie Imazu and Bill Wellman.

Lunch on location.

The Smith family: Joe, Mary, and young Johnny.

FOREWORD

I have always wanted to do a book which would state realistically and in detail how a motion picture is made. I had reserved this plan for some time in the future, when other men will be doing the work I am now doing, and when I would be able to look back and reflect on the enjoyable effort of most of my lifetime.

However, the making of the film, *The Next Voice You Hear*, was so stimulating that it propelled me into attempting this job long before I actually had the full time to do it. Help came along in the form of one Charles Palmer, an experienced, capable writer who tackles his assignments with the wide-eyed enthusiasm of an apprentice who has just sold his first byline to the local gazette. "Cap" (for his initials) shares my enthusiasm for films, knows his way around the studios, and has skill and experience with the printed word. He was willing to take on this collaborative and "as told to" assignment, and I am delighted he did, because even though I have not been able to write all of this book, it is exactly the way I would have wanted to write it. Cap did most of the putting together of the words from notes taken at sessions we had during free hours in the morning, or at night, or on Sundays; from some articles I had worked on; some speeches I had made; from my own dictated comments and handwritten scrawls—and finally, from his own keen eye and his own talent.

DORE SCHARY

PART ONE

The Story and the Script

1

We had just previewed a picture out at the pleasant little Bay Theatre in Pacific Palisades. Afterward the people from the studio were gathered out front under the lighted marquee. There was the usual relieved kidding and congratulations and cross-talk that follows a successful showing. The two new stars who had just been born were the targets of everyone's friendly curiosity.

But my own eyes drifted to a drab, unobtrusive object sitting on the curb waiting for a pickup car to take it back to the studio. It looked like an octagonal galvanized film can, battered and fringed with the shreds of old shipping labels, but actually it was a sort of jewel box. In it were the days and nights, the thought and sweat of a lot of wonderful people; in it were the hopes and fears and perhaps the careers of those people. There were new homes and the means for sending boys and girls to college. And in it, too, were the images which, when threaded through the projectors of the world, would bring entertainment and pleasure, perhaps a new emotional experience, perhaps even a change of heart to many millions of people, perhaps to you.

Now and in the foreseeable future, images on films are going to be a principal influence on our hearts and emotions and minds. We ought to know more about it. And so I want to tell you the step-by-step story of exactly how a feature motion picture is made, from the author's germ idea to the floodlit premiere.

The film in that octagonal can happened to be the work-print of a picture called *The Next Voice You Hear.* It is a very simple picture, almost "basic," and all the steps and functions of film production stand out clearly. By seeing how this one picture was made we can get a pretty good idea of how all pictures are made.

More than any other form of art or entertainment, movies are of the people, by the people and for the people. "Of" in the sense of being about people, real people, whom audiences recognize as true; "for" in the sense that the picture truly exists only when it is being viewed by the people of the audience; and "by" in the sense that any one picture is a sum total of the minds and muscles of a great many contributors.

A painting or a statue or a book is usually a one-man production. But a movie script is more like the score of a symphony. The written notes of the symphony mean little until men play them in concert, and a movie script can be transferred from the paper to the screen only by the creative contributions of many hard-working and talented men and women. The motion picture is the most collaborative of all the arts.

And this collaboration goes all the way; for a picture takes on its full dimension only when it is being shown to an audience. A picture is a chronicle of emotion, and that emotion is half on the screen and half in the response of the people who see it, the people who identify themselves with it as it unfolds. The audience is the Pygmalion which brings the celluloid Galatea to life.

Therefore, this book is about all of us. We, the makers; you, the audience.

2

The starting point of a story, any story, from *Humpty Dumpty* to *War and Peace,* is somebody's idea; a germ idea which somebody considers promising enough to justify the effort of filling and fleshing and building it out into a form ready for the public's judgment. Perhaps you're right to start the project, perhaps you're wrong; you won't find out for sure until later. At the idea stage, you think it's good and you will of necessity go through the same steps with the same fervor for a great success as for a resounding flop. Like raising a child.

The germ ideas which grow into motion pictures are often very simple. Usually they can be expressed in the length of a telegram. And usually they come from simple beginnings. The trick is to recognize them.

One noontime in the spring of 1948, in Wilmington, Delaware, author George Sumner Albee was lunching with a Dr. Morris. The two men got to chatting about the state of the world, particularly man's misuse of certain scientific miracles. Something suddenly struck Albee funny; he grinned and remarked that one of these miracles might be used to advantage. "You know," he said, "wouldn't it be something if God would come on the radio and give people such a bad scare they'd wake up and behave themselves!" Morris laughed and, over coffee, the two of them dreamed up a lot of miracles which might do the waking. But it wasn't until a few evenings later that Albee recog-

nized it as the germ idea of a story. He was spending
the evening in New York with his friend Dale Eunson, fiction editor of *Cosmopolitan Magazine*, and ribbing Eunson
pleasantly about the reluctance of magazines to print stories
with originality. "For instance?" Eunson challenged. Albee
hesitated a second, then remembered the conversation about
God coming on the radio. "We'd use that," said Eunson.
"You write it and we'll buy it." Fortunately, Albee then
caught a cold which sent him to bed for four days and gave
him time to think out the story. The time seems short, but
the germ idea was so lucidly simple and concise that it did
not need complicated plotting, only to be dressed with
incident and circumstance. Albee's literary agent read the
manuscript and said it was so bad she would not even sub-
mit it to the magazine editors. But by now Albee was so
confident that the story said something which needed saying
that he got himself a new agent, breaking a friendship of a
decade in the process, and transmitted the story to Dale
Eunson. *Cosmopolitan* bought the story the next morning,
and ran it in their issue of August, 1948.

Albee deposited the check, said thanks to various readers
who said pleasant things about the story, and figured that
was probably that. He thought of a film sale, naturally, but
several important incidents of the story such as the sinking
of the continent of Australia presented such obvious technical difficulties that a movie seemed out of the question.
However, the simple fact of publication of the story had
started certain wheels in motion.

One set of these wheels was housed on the opposite side
of the continent, in the Metro-Goldwyn-Mayer Administration Building. The studios cover about seventy-five

acres in Culver City, California, a few miles southwest of Hollywood on the flatlands down toward the beach. They don't look particularly romantic: the massed ranks of the twenty-five stages look more like huge warehouses, their windowless walls rising like gray stucco cliffs above the thirteen miles of narrow concrete streets enclosed within the boundary fences. Around the core of stages are the long open-shed scene docks, the wooden lofts and corrugated-iron shacks of the shop colony, a lake-like "tank" where half of a tramp steamer is moored next to a Roman galley.

The Administration Building, four stories of white concrete set in green lawn, is located at the east end of the production lot and is known because of its air-conditioning system as the Iron Lung. In its four hundred offices are housed the company executives, the lawyers, the several producers, the writers, and Kenneth MacKenna's Story Department, to which in June of 1948 as a matter of everyday routine came the advance proof of the *Cosmopolitan* issue containing *The Next Voice You Hear*. Dorothy Pratt sifted through the morning's grist on her desk and assigned the story to one of the fifteen story analysts in her department. The analyst drew off a synopsis, put down a personal opinion, and relayed the file along the corridor to editor Marjorie Thorson.

These synopses are designed to capture the producer's interest and give him the essential bones of the stories: they provide the only means by which an executive can even begin to cover the field in the hours (usually the late night hours) he can set aside for his reading. When a synopsis intrigues him he calls for the original book or story or play and reads it in full. Often our reader's synopsis, particularly

of a long novel, is better than the original for our purposes;
crisper, the story line cleaner, and the characters standing
out in sharper relief.

Most Metro readers and sub-editors come to the studio
direct from college, where they had majored in literature
and achieved a sufficient fluency in at least one language to
read foreign story material in the original. All of them have
broad human interests and good cultural backgrounds; most
of them have traveled. Readers are paid from sixty-five
dollars to one hundred twenty-five dollars per week, and
in the course of a single year they and their counterparts
in the Loew's offices in New York, Paris and London synop-
size almost twenty-five thousand pieces of material. Since
they read much of it in publishers' advance proofs, they
know long ahead of time how the magazine serials come
out.

Strangely, despite the avalanche of plays and novels and
magazine stories and manuscript "screen originals," it is not
easy to find the thirty to fifty stories on which the studio
must build its year's production. The fact is, when we buy
a story we virtually open up a new business in which we
will invest a capital of from several hundred thousand dollars up to three or four million. Therefore we ask quite a
lot from a story before we buy it.

First of all, a story must be "for us"; it must fit our program, permit practical casting, and generally be ready to
go. But it must also have wide appeal to all kinds of people,
it must be adaptable to visual telling, contain fresh pictorial
elements to satisfy the audience eye, must be built around
strong and intriguing characters (preferably with a good
part for one of our contract stars), permit telling on the
screen in not much more than ninety minutes, be non-topi-

cal enough not to "date" before we get our investment back. And it must sparkle with enough of that intangible called showmanship to make millions of people hurry through their dinners on a rainy night and park too far from an overcrowded theatre because they just can't wait another day. This is an ideal, I'll admit, but we always try for the brass ring.

Oddly, the Story Department does not so much buy stories as "sell" them—that is, bring them to the attention of the studio's producers who must select stories for the pictures they make. When the synopsis on *Next Voice* came down the line, the editors were sufficiently intrigued to read the whole version; which, since the original was a short story, was attached in full. When they had read it they found themselves tantalized, because any story which caught their interest so sharply would surely have a chance to catch the interest of the millions outside. But they had to admit that the conversion of the story to the screen offered great difficulties, and when the producers who had seen the synopsis agreed, the story was regretfully shelved.

This took place a month or so before I came into Metro as head of Production. It happened that I came across *Next Voice* independently, in a copy of *Cosmopolitan* which I picked up to read on the train coming home from New York. My reaction was the same as that of the editors: I loved the idea and didn't know how to do it. When I checked in at the studio I talked the story over with Kenneth MacKenna and we decided to try to buy it anyway, gambling on the chance that we could find a way to beat the problem. But the price turned out to be higher than we thought we should invest on such a long shot, and the project went on the shelf the second time, apparently for good,

That was in September of 1948. I thought of the story off and on for the next year, with a lack of ideas which began to grow embarrassing. Then one morning it broke open.

3

The term "producer" has many meanings in Hollywood. I will be talking here about only the real producers, the men who truly contribute to their pictures and to the industry, who try to do a job rather than hold one. Even so, the species has many variations.

Some producers, like Sam Goldwyn, own their own studios. Others, like Hal Wallis, are semi-independent, in that they own their own production companies but use the physical facilities, distribution services, and often the financing of the major companies. Most producers, however, are employees of a large studio who carry the management responsibility for individual pictures.

In essence, a producer is a man who starts with an idea or hope and ends with a completed picture ready for the screen. The idea may be an actual germ of a new story, or it may be the obstinate belief that an existing property like *The Next Voice You Hear* can somehow be made into a successful movie.

The public has heard of a few producers like Selznick, Zanuck, Goldwyn and DeMille, but except for a lot of bad jokes they have only the foggiest idea of what a producer really does. Actually it's not at all mysterious. He's the "head man" of a given film enterprise. It is the producer who hires or assigns the writer, the director and the other varied talent, and, acting as founder and general manager of the project, guides and co-ordinates these talents until he comes out at the far end with a film sufficiently alluring and satisfying to a worldwide audience to bring its investment back with a profit. Sometimes a less active routine is followed, in which case our hero becomes an ex-producer, often very swiftly. Usually he is a rather positive character and his pictures will all tend to reflect a "point of view" which becomes his style. I've noticed a common denominator in all of the successful producers: they all love the actual routine of making pictures; in fact, they're usually a little stagestruck.

Usually, the producer's only hobby is the picture business, if only because that's all he has time for. He can never admit that there is such a word as "final": he is constantly re-examining everything about his project, eternally looking for those minor improvements which may add up to make an adequate picture into a good or great one. Unfortunately, this process is not self-stopping upon the completion of the picture, and he is probably a little unhappy about everything he has ever done.

I've mentioned that I had not been able to get that *Next Voice* story idea out of my mind. It was a superb story for a magazine; the printed story happens in the reader's imagination, it plays before your mind's eye and you can alter the imaginary image to suit your own taste. But a movie plays before your physical eye, and we can show you only one picture at a time and that picture must have specific reality. Those intriguing miracles of Albee's—the sinking of the continent of Australia, the growing of angel's wings on the atheists, etc.—just wouldn't work on the screen. The sinking of Australia on film would obviously be a "special effects" miniature sequence, and the actual photograph of feathered wings growing on some of our actors would just be funny. But above and beyond these matters of mechanics, I felt very strongly that the God I worship wouldn't perform this particular kind of miracle; he wouldn't flaunt his power, he wouldn't humiliate his children. I felt that, for film, the story should be built around a wholly different kind of miracle. I didn't know what kind.

And there was another problem: a very serious problem of dramatics. The printed story began with the effect of God's radio words on the members of one family, but as the events of the story progressed the first characters were left behind and new characters were touched on, until at the end the cast included the population of the world.

In the magazine it was very effective. But we have found from long experience, some of it unhappy, that the core of a successful picture is its characters. From beginning to end, the film must follow the fortunes of one, two or three people about whom the audience is sure to feel strongly, and it's best that the audience be sympathetic, that they love the people and perhaps identify themselves with them and be glad when things turn out well for them in the end. In the words of the old industry bromide, to which you, the audience, always demands a satisfying answer, "who will we be rooting for?" Again, I didn't know.

Then one night, a year after the story had been shelved, a tantalizing shadow of an idea drifted into my mind. I couldn't pin it down, but the next morning I woke up about six with the story still in my mind and feeling as though it were about to break. There seemed to be a clue in a parallel situation of some years ago when I had read Paul Gallico's *Joe Smith, American* and been equally puzzled about how to convert it into a picture. We had found a way to lick that

problem; if I could recapture that old thought process perhaps the same approach would beat this one. I kept thinking
about Joe Smith, Joe Smith . . . We've got to bring this
cosmic thing down to simple terms, a real story about real
people to whom God will seem real. . . .

Then came the break. Why not let God speak on the
radio to Joe Smith himself? Give Joe the same kind of a
wife and son he had in the earlier picture, the same typical
middle-class American environment, the same petty annoy-
ances that would seem so big until something bigger than the
physical world came back into his life. The idea began to
shape itself, to take on color.

What about the problem of the miracles? As so often
happens, the good things in a story come when you have to
go to work and fill in the holes. Here, we'd fill in the hole
with truth, the film-story miracles would be those that had
always been around Joe but which he'd stopped noticing;
the sun and the moon and the rain, and growth, and the
astounding miracle of birth. Automatically, this supplied a
destination for the events in our story; the goal would be
Joe's realization. The action would be the events which
caused Joe ultimately to open his eyes to these miracles and
to learn to create for himself new miracles of love and kind-
ness and peace.

The producer's best insurance for a long productive
life is a split personality in which the artistic is balanced by
the practical. The concept was now complete, and it had
all the qualities needed to make a creditable picture. But,
came the practical question—could this picture go out into
the theatres and earn its living?

It would be a gamble, a very long one. It would be a

gamble in money and reputation. We're used to that, but this gamble went further. Many of us in the industry have long believed that decent people doing good things could be made dramatically interesting and exciting, and that the public would accept such pictures. The commercial failure of *The Next Voice* could be a serious setback to that whole point of view.

Although there is no such thing as a "sure-fire" picture, a fact which the industry rediscovers expensively at intervals, the outlook for most pictures can be estimated in the light of our experience with past pictures of the same type which have done well or done badly. A big western, for example, is more or less a staple commodity. If your new one has a fresh approach, a well-constructed story, a competent director and proven stars, you have a fair basis for estimating whether the proposed budget will be recovered with a profit. And without profit on some pictures to balance your losses on others, you and the studio employees who depend on you for jobs are soon going to be out of same.

⸙ With *The Next Voice*, all we had to go on were the axioms that "message" pictures drive people away from the theatres, and religion is poison at the box-office. We would have both. Balancing these considerations was the conviction that we could make a whale of an interesting and exciting picture; that in the present disturbed state of the world a lot of people needed the assurance and comfort that this story could bring, and that if you supply a real need you usually somehow get compensated for it. Also, any showman is bound to have in the back of his mind the tempting realization that it's often the gambling pictures which make the smashes: still fresh in my own mind was the success of

Battleground, the first film to break through the latest of
the recurring taboos against pictures about war.

 ⊢ It's part of the job of an executive to make decisions; he's
supposed to have enough experience and judgment to make
more right ones than wrong ones. And make them he must,
quickly and cleanly, resisting the temptation to draw comfort and protection—and delay—from too much counsel-
ing and temporizing. The next time you envy some highly
paid executive in the steel business or automobile manufacturing or the movie industry, you might remember that a
simple little "We'll do it" from him may put in motion the
spending of millions of dollars and risk the security of a lot
of people who depend on his judgment for their daily income. The responsibility can be very heavy. And it gets
lonely out there on the limb.

I laid out in my own mind certain approaches to the project which would minimize the gamble, and asked Kenneth
MacKenna to see about buying the picture rights to Mr.
Albee's original story. Our New York office wired that they
could get together with the literary agent on price. Schary
the executive took a deep breath, hoped he was right, and
said to Schary the producer, "We'll do it."

4

There was a wonderful old vaudeville act in which the solo actor played several parts, the gimmick being that when he changed characters he changed hats. The producer in pictures has a hat rack that will stack up against anybody's, and probably the hat he uses most often if the one labeled Salesman.

The author sells the original story once. The producer sells it many, many times. For example, the fundamental picture which I had in mind, the approach which might justify the gamble, would stand or fall on the director. The slightest touch of staginess would ruin the picture; every move and word of Joe Smith and everybody around him would have to be utterly real. And the picture would have to be pushed through on a shooting schedule so short that most "quality" directors would consider it impossible. I wanted Bill Wellman. We had worked together very happily on *Battleground:* pictures all the way from *Wings* and *A Star Is Born* proved him a magnificent director of realism. He's a rabid family man, feels things deeply, and is completely honest. Billy has great ability and experience in the business, and is a man of enormous enthusiasm: if he would catch fire on the idea and agree to gamble his reputation on a short schedule, we'd be well along. I asked him to come up to the office.

He sat down by the desk, fixed me with a skeptical blue eye, and the butterflies which always live in producers' stomachs began to beat their wings. I opened, "Billy, I've got a notion . . ." and gave him the nub of the idea. Fortunately, there's a lot of Joe Smith in Wellman's personal philosophy. He got the idea before I had finished telling it and characteristically shoved his whole pile of chips out into the middle of the table. The butterflies took a short nap.

Now the bare idea would have to be built up into a rounded story, and then into a detailed screen play which Wellman could shoot. How would it be done? Well, you can't pin down the creative process into a step-by-step routine in the germ stage of a story; you take what your subconscious flips up to the surface and put the pieces together. But you do know, from experience, what pieces you need to put together into a story structure.

We had the central situation—"God talks on the radio." Our theme flowed logically out of that. "If everybody behaved well toward each other we'd drive out envy, hate and contempt, and be a lot better off." We had our characters—a father, mother and young son of a typical "Joe Smith, American" family. Our physical locale flowed naturally from the characters—an FHA bungalow with a mortgage, a neighborhood to suit, an aircraft plant where Joe worked, and so on. All this was raw material for the events which would have to be invented to bring the theme home to the characters and fulfill the purpose of the story.

We also had our problems. Somehow we had to fill the hole left by eliminating the sensational miracles of the printed story. We'd fill it with the "everyday miracles" which the story would bring our characters to see and realize. We needed a structure, a physical plan in which the events of the story would be arranged: Mr. Albee's printed story had been divided into the seven days of the Biblical Creation, and the same plan would work out splendidly for us. But there was still the problem of the Voice.

People frequently ask, "Why do the movies always change the stories they buy?" Well, we don't, unless we have to. We would dearly love to film books and plays and printed stories exactly as they are; we'd save a great deal of money in script cost and have some time for golf. But it just isn't possible. Oftentimes, important segments of the story which were very effective in the original medium simply don't come off when you take pictures of them. It isn't quite true that, "You can't take a picture of a thought," but obviously the film medium is a visual one. The crux is, film is specific; everybody who looks at a screen sees exactly the same picture and hears exactly the same words. Our dilemma about how to handle the Voice illustrated one facet of the problem.

In the printed story, God's Voice spoke and the characters heard it: you read the words the Voice spoke and you heard it, too. But you heard it in your imagination, and so it could be a wonderful Voice that was fitting to the way you think of God. Your neighbor "heard" an entirely different Voice. But what happens when we carry the same thing over into the film medium? First, we would have to hire an actor to impersonate the Voice of God. This would rightly be considered presumptuous and irreverent. It would also sound completely phony. Of course, we could put the actor's voice through filters and reverberation chambers, underscore it with ethereal music, superimpose clouds over the radio set and so on through the whole bag

of tricks. But we all felt, from our varied religious points
of view, that this picture had no place for tricks or devices.
There was only one logical conclusion to us: we would
never actually hear the Voice.

At first glance it would seem that this pulled the keystone out of the whole structure. But again the lash of necessity compelled new thinking which worked out to the
advantage of the picture. We would capitalize our disad-
vantage by inventing action which would prevent us from
hearing the Voice, and try to make that action so interesting
that the audience would never feel we were ducking the
issue. Of course, we would have to invent a different piece
of voice-blocking action for each one of the seven nights
—and here, ready-made, was our "floor plan"—the starting
point for our story thinking.

This was in November of 1949. I had to go to New York
for the opening of *Battleground*, and by the time I got back
home the idea was filling out into the shape of a story. The
subconscious had come up with good visual reasons for not
hearing the Voice on the first and second nights, and also on
the last night—which, added the fleshing-out process, would
logically take place in a crowded church. The "everyday
miracle" which would pervade the story could be only one
—the miracle of birth. Joe's and Mary's baby would be
born on the seventh night, and the birth would contribute
the climax of the picture.

Now, although there was much left to do, the destination
had come out in the clear and the road to it was apparent.
It was time for me to call in a screen writer. For the record,
it should be stated that the writer generally comes on a
project at a much earlier stage. But I earned my living at
the craft for a long time, and on a picture which I produce

personally I can't conscientiously start a writer on salary until I have set up a story line I know will work. I asked Milton Beecher, who handles our salaried writers, to check on the availability of a young man named Charles Schnee.

5

There is no such thing as a typical screen writer except in cartoons, but Charlie Schnee is reasonably representative. Contrary to the cartoons, his coat and trousers usually match, but he does wear the characteristic horn-rimmed glasses and goes in for strange shoes. Typically, he got into the profession of screen writing by accident; he graduated from Yale Law School in 1939, and while waiting for the results of his bar exams, wrote a play. I wanted him for this picture because he's a fellow with great feeling and this would be a highly emotional story. I have found also that he stimulates my own thinking in a conference, stirs me up, and I knew that he was secure enough in his job to call things as he saw them rather than accept a bad idea because the producer thought it was great. Also we had him under contract and he was approaching the finish of his current assignment.

Just before Thanksgiving I called Charlie up to the office. I said, "I've got a notion, see what you think. . . ." and I told him the idea of God speaking on the radio, the Joe Smith adaptation, and the scattered pieces which had so far attached themselves to the story. Charlie wiped away a tear at the finish, but I wasn't too sold because Charlie's capacity for feeling deeply sometimes makes him cry at card tricks. I asked him to think about it for the next three days in a general way.

He dropped in for a minute or two in mid-week to say

THE STORY AND THE SCRIPT

that it felt good and he'd like to take on the assignment. At the end of the week he came in for a meeting with his first ideas for building out the story.

It was pretty well established by now that the emotional line of the story would be fear, mortal fear which would key the reawakening of our characters to the freedom from fear which awaits them in God. So Charlie's ideas tended to demonstrate that theme. He had thought of Johnny, the young son, becoming frightened and running away. In a search for conflict and a means for causing fear in Joe, he had thought of the factory foreman character, Mr. Brannan. He was exploring the idea of a fear that Mary's pregnancy would end in trouble (which later turned out as the false-labor incident), and he wondered about the notion of bringing in a temptation for Joe, which later developed into the bar sequence. Between us, we now had the incidents for each of the seven nights which would prevent the actual hearing of the Voice. Lucy Ballentine, my top secretarial assistant, brought her book into the office and we dictated the first approach to what the Voice would say each night.

A week later Charlie came out to the house in the evening. The projectionist ran off the 1941 *Joe Smith, American* to refresh us on the characters and circumstances. Mrs. Schary urged Jill, Joy and Jeb off to bed, Lucy got out her book, and we started pinning down the story. A columnist later said the story was written in three hours. It was dictated in three hours; there's a vast difference.

When a writer spends several weeks on an assignment without turning in a page and then sets the whole story down on paper in a few days, he is not necessarily guilty of high-priced loafing. And often when a writer says, "It's all finished except for the writing," he is not trying to be

funny. The whole story or play or picture has been worked
out in his mind and needs only to be copied down on the
paper.

This one evening at the house was simply the crystalliza-
tion of a year's thinking, some of it conscious and a lot of it
that wonderful free ride which the subconscious mind gives
to a project which locks its interest. But the final dictation
went with the smoothness that often blesses the truly simple
story; we filled our need for some physical manifestation
of God's power with the idea of the on-cue rainstorm, and
at one o'clock in the morning Lucy closed her book. We
sat around for a while in the den, with that pleasantly
drained feeling which follows a tense run, talked a little
about the casting of the picture, and then Charlie started
along home. I went out to his car with him and as I walked
back toward the house I looked up at the stars and had the
odd feeling that I knew them better than when I'd come
home a few short hours ago.

Two days later, over lunch in my suite at the studio
(it was frankfurters and baked beans, the luxury in this
business is fabulous), Bill Wellman, Charlie and I read the
thirty typed pages of yellow paper which made up the
story treatment. We agreed that it would work. Bill began
to see what he could do with it in the way of directorial
touches, and went out on the limb with a guarantee that it
could be shot on a schedule so short as to be considered
fantastic. The treatment was sufficiently detailed for Charlie
to figure he could cut the time for writing the screen play
down to four weeks.

It's one thing to prepare a picture, and another to persuade the authorities to place it on the schedule. But Schary
the producer put the case to Schary the executive in coura-

geous man-to-man fashion, no holds barred, and came out with the green light. I notified the Production Department that we could be ready to go around March first, and to set the picture up on their schedules.

Ostensibly because the project was a dangerous gamble, but actually because the lot of us saw a chance to have some professional fun, *Next Voice* became a test case for reducing some of the high costs which have plagued the industry in recent years. You can cut costs in one of two general ways. One way is to reduce arbitrarily all expenditures, using less of everything, including talent. The other way is to substitute thought for money. Often the pleasant result of the latter is that the goading of your ingenuity and imagination make the picture not only cheaper but better. If what happens between two people in a scene is strong enough you can play it in front of a board fence, and if you can't use money for an eye-filling set you can go to work and build up the emotional content of the scene.

The Next Voice was already committed to simple locales and action. And although Charlie would write in enough sets for visual variety, he would make sure that each set backed enough of the action to buy its way into the picture. For example, we wouldn't plan a 100-yard traveling shot along a factory corridor when we could have Joe make the same plot points while he changed his shoes in a corner of a locker room. However, if our story had actually contained important plot action that had to be played in the expensive travel shot to put over an essential point, we'd line it up cheerfully and without stinting. It's all a question of values.

For certain functional purposes a silk handkerchief

doesn't deliver any more value than a cotton one. What we wanted to get rid of here was waste and extravagance, to apportion our available money to expenditures which would go all the way through to the screen and deliver full value to the audience.

6

Charlie Schnee took the thirty yellow pages home to convert our treatment into a screen play.

The treatment, as you have seen, is simply a rough sketch of the proposed picture: most screen originals which we buy for filming are in treatment form. Screen writers are constantly being asked by outside writers just how a treatment should be set up, what is the proper typographical format, how many pages should it run, and so on. The fact is, there is no form; you simply tell the story; who the characters are, what they want, what's blocking the way, and how they go about achieving their goal. The proper length is the fewest number of pages needed to make the essence of the story clear and interesting—and to bring out unmistakably the essential "kernel of appeal," which is going to make those millions of people hurry to the theatre to see this particular picture. And it's expected that the action will be "in the medium," thought out with an eye to how it will look and sound on the screen, and practical to shoot.

From the physical side, Charlie's job was now to convert thirty pages of close-typed prose into approximately one hundred "sides" of screen play, expressed in dialogue and instructions. The job would call not only for creative writing talent, but for a technique equivalent to that possessed by an architect, attorney, or other professional practitioner.

Up to this stage of a picture, some of the participants

may have been able to complete their statements with a
wave of the hand and "You see what I mean." But there
would now be no room for vagueness.

The screen writer's first step is to reach an explicit crys-
tallization in his mind as to which character is the lead, just
what the story is about, and exactly where it is going. With
this as a backbone he now goes through his material, dis-
carding whatever does not sharply develop the characters
and move the story along the straight line to its goal, and
relating everything else to that line.

He must invent threads of action and reaction and "business" to visualize those thoughts of which we can't take
pictures and to give his characters the stuff of life, then
weave these threads in and out of the scenes, embroidering
the straightforward progress of the plot, so that scenes
take on relationship to each other and eventually weave
into a pattern of over-all unity. He must find ways to in-
troduce his important people characteristically and memo-
rably without being obvious about it.

He must invent brief transitions to take the place of
lengthy dull sequences, and many points must be "planted."
For some reason, certain actions are funnier, more dramatic,
or whatever, if the way has been subtly prepared so that the
unexpected seems logical. In *Next Voice* the laugh when the
motorcycle cop catches Joe slamming back out of his driveway into the street is much bigger because we've already
seen Joe back out too fast before (the "plant") and we
know sometime he's going to get caught at it. And the
plant was kept from being obvious by being made funny
in itself, when Joe backed out almost into another driver and
the two yelled insults at each other like good American
motorists.

Everything the screen writer does he must test against two standards: the words "simple" and "inevitable." He must find economical scenes to visualize what the original author nonchalantly disposed of with the impractical word "gradually." He must, particularly, distill and distill and combine and combine, until each scene of his final script has brevity and power and quickness, telling whole pages of dialogue in a single momentary exchange. The continuity of his piece must be on the screen, not on the sound track, if it's fully to utilize the power of the medium, and everything that happens must be arranged in a logical sequence of cause and effect so that at any point in the script he can say, "Given these people, under these pressures, what is happening here is inevitable."

The writer may put a job through several versions, each one somewhat clearer and more refined, more of its nonessentials stripped away. And the point at which he knows his work is finished is the point at which he gets no credit for what he has done, when the piece has been refined down to such inevitable simplicity that the onlookers' reaction is, "It was a soft job—only one way he could possibly write it."

The *Next Voice* job was more rugged than some because it would depend for a lot of its impact on intriguing bits of circumstance and character action. That sort of thing is harder to get hold of than the "plotty" picture where clearly definable good guys slug it out with equally unmistakable bad guys for the grazing rights, West Side beer monopoly, atom-plane plans, or the love of a good woman. This story would happen inside peoples' minds and hearts. On the other hand, our existing story treatment was more than usually detailed and there were fewer holes.

Charlie decided to work at home rather than at the studio, and he handed in the first third of the screen play at the end of the first week. We worked on some changes, but I told him I liked the approach and to keep on going as he was headed. He turned in the second third eight days later, and after a few more sessions the whole ninety-five pages went down to the mimeographs in Edith Farrell's Script Department three days under his four-week deadline.

Screen writers sooner or later become resigned to the fact that the appearance of their first draft is greeted with, "Fine. Now we've got something to change." Which is healthy, within reasonable limits, because every specialist who applies his particular talent to a picture ought to "plus" it. Wellman and I had some changes; Billy in particular had a number of improvements later on. There were no deep structural alterations. But before the script could be stamped "completed" and shoved out into the stream, it had to be scrutinized by three highly specialized departments.

While everyone else is striving to make a film authentic in every tiny detail, Ruth de Saxe and her girls in the Legal Research Department are inching methodically through the script and planting therein a score of intentional inaccuracies. There is a mistaken idea that the appearance of one's face, name, property, telephone number, or whatever, on a theatre screen automatically entitles one after a few legal preliminaries to a life-long pension in compensation for this invasion of privacy. Hence, Ruth tries to make sure that "any similarity to actual persons . . . is purely coincidental."

For instance, the script gave the name "Fred Brannan" to Joe's boss, a crotchety old man and an atheist. We checked

Douglas Aircraft, where the sequence would be photographed, and found that while there were some fifty employees named "Brannon" or "Brannan" or "Brannen" in their three local plants, none was employed as a foreman, either on the active or inactive list. An Atlas Aircraft Company was found to be in legal existence, so we changed ours to Ajax and made employees' badges accordingly, filling the extras' badges with names like "Dibson" which did not appear in any Los Angeles directories or reference books. Then, though we cleared the name "HOPSY TOPSY" for the repaint job on a rented Good Humor ice-cream truck, its chimes gave trouble: the Music Department okayed Good Humor's "Little Brown Jug" as in public domain, but reminded us that any accompanying chords or noodles would constitute an "arrangement," probably protected by copyright. And the radio call letters KIH which we thought we had invented turned out to be in use by an Alaskan Coastal Harbor Station; the FCC finally cleared the letters KWTA.

Though we would often like to use actual brand names of various products to help project an atmosphere of reality, manufacturers resent our giving a "plug" to a competitor's product and theatregoers wonder if we are being paid for the ad. Legal's list of brand names which sound authentic but do not exist include such seemingly familiar products as Lubeck Beer, Templeton Cigarettes, Solax film, Barkwell Dog Food, and Chickering Tires. We recently had to throw away a wonderful whisky label because a real distiller liked our brand name and started using it.

There was a breakfast cereal in the *Next Voice* opening scene which went through various stages from JOYS to CHEERS, GUSTOS, ZESTS, TREATS and GLEES. The Patent

Office reported every name but GLEES to be registered for
use as an actual trademark. I'll never forget the reaction
of the team to that last suggestion. Charlie Schnee frowned,
I swallowed hard, and Wellman cut loose with a yelp of
pure outrage, "GLEES! What kind of a kid would eat GLEES!"

Everybody finally got together on HAPPIES, and Props
started making up the dummy boxes. Props also made up
the metal badge for the motorcycle officer, but only after
Legal had insisted on changing the lettering "Los Angeles"
to "LA" to guard against the badge getting out of the
studio into the hands of some unscrupulous person who
might open up his own police business on the strength of
it.

◁ To the Censorship Department, *Next Voice* was a brand-
new kind of problem. They have well-established standards
for judging Esther Williams bathing suits and Lana Turner
love scenes (this is generally considered by others on the
lot to be pleasant work), but there were no precedents for
our pregnancy angle. Yet when a vital plot point requires
that your heroine have a baby seven days from your opening scene, you just can't tiptoe through the tulips. There
was also a serious question about the reaction by religious
groups to our lack of formality in speaking about God.

We put both matters up to Joseph Breen, who administers
the self-policing code of the industry. He saw nothing vital
that would be offensive, if filmed with honest intent and in
good taste. But he did go on record with warnings that local
censorship boards in various parts of the country would
object to certain specific items. So we changed the words
"jerk" and "lousy," skirted specific verbal reference to
"pains," and made some other unimportant changes.

But it was also suggested that we eliminate Mary's curtain line, when she leaves the hospital after the false labor: "I feel like such a fool, leaving here just as big as when I came in." We felt that line was so human and so characteristic—and entirely decent in its spirit—that we decided to risk trouble with local censorship boards and leave it in. Any power of censorship has serious implications to the whole idea of individual freedom. As a practical matter, we bow to it a good share of the time, to prevent local tampering with our pictures, but occasions arise when you have to say, "This is the way it's got to be," and battle it out.✹

This credo cracked into an all-or-nothing test when we sent the script down to Bob Vogel's International Department. Bob broke down the script with the knowledge that it might be translated into twenty-eight languages for distribution in fifty-six foreign countries. One of his twin responsibilities is to make the action intelligible to people unfamiliar with many American customs. For instance, although foreign audiences would never understand the fine points of the baseball sequences in last year's *Stratton Story*, Bob had to make sure they would always know at least whether our hero was doing fine or in danger. For another instance, he asked us to change the word "tabloid" in our script, since in Britain that is a copyrighted word which means not a newspaper, but a certain brand of pill. But a more serious problem is worldwide censorship. He is concerned with a maze of moral, religious, political, and nobody-knows-why taboos which overflow the eight typewritten volumes on his desk.

Ordinarily, Vogel works up a list of changes which may

render certain objectionable bits of the picture acceptable
to various of the foreign markets. Sometimes we can amend
the American version so that it will be acceptable elsewhere;
sometimes we will shoot a given scene two ways. Obviously,
we have to re-shoot any printed material which we want a
foreign audience to read, which is why you usually see a
book or a piece of music in close-up "insert" with little or
no background.

But the foreign censorship problem on *Next Voice* went
far beyond the stage of minor changes. Bob had our London
office check the script with the authorities in England, the
market which would account for most of our foreign gross,
and got back the informal advice that we were, in effect,
dead. In justice, it must be admitted that the whole tempo
of British life is on a more formal basis than ours, and the
informal, intimate acceptance by Joe and Mary and Johnny
of God as a part of everyday life and conversation seemed
to them sacrilegious. Against this view there would be no
hope of compromise through "protection" shots, because
the objection went to the core of the whole story, the
characters, the theme, and the atmosphere.

This was serious. Despite the difficulty in bringing our
earnings back to this country, the British gross has in the
past usually represented our full profit on a picture. And
so we could either drop the project, or we could reinforce
our determination to drive the picture through under such
economical procedures that we would have a chance to
recover our investment from the domestic market alone.
We decided to take our chance on the domestic gross.

On February 2nd the script covers were changed from
"temporary" blue to "hit the road" yellow. There would be
more changes, on the usual vari-colored revision pages—

the only way to freeze a script is to freeze your mind—but the changes from here on would not affect the production flow. The Accounting Department assigned Production Number 1488, and the trim little messenger girls spread out from the Script Department with the 115 mimeographed copies of the screenplay which would automatically set in motion the complicated machinery of producing a movie.

PART TWO

Preparation for Production

7

The distribution of the yellow-covered scripts placed the picture officially in the hands of the Production lot. But there were still some limbs to be crawled out on over on the Executive side. The riskiest limb involved a policy decision on casting—would we cast Joe and Mary with stars or unknowns?

Sixty percent of all movie tickets are bought "to see my favorite star." Even adult moviegoers of real discrimination deduce from the name of the star what general type of film an unfamiliar title probably represents. For good or ill, the demand of the American public has brought the star system into being. A young extra gets a few feet of film in *Pilot No. 5*, people write in to ask his name, we give him a bit or two and the mail increases, and Peter Lawford moves from obscurity toward the star list.

Contrary to a general impression, we do not have the power to pick up just anybody from a gas pump or perfume counter and make him or her into a star. Of course we can teach a girl to act, to dress, and all the rest of it, but if she didn't happen to be born with that indefinable twist of personality which "jumps off the screen and takes hold of you," nothing we can do will make the public buy tickets to a picture mostly because she's in it.

Since 1924 when Loew's bought the Goldwyn plant and engaged Mr. Mayer to manage their Metro production company, M-G-M has followed the policy of growing its

own stars from seed rather than buying them after they
have hit. Today blonde, crisp Lucille Ryman is the gateway
to tomorrow's star material. To her office come tips, photos,
recommendations, and applications from literally every-
where—including a crop of letters from lame-duck senators
after each election. She even holds open auditions, and a
youngster who shows any promise of having that personality spark will be turned over to dramatic coach Lillian
Burns for development. The newcomer will be coached
in drama, voice, dancing, deportment, eurythmics, dress,
makeup, manners, and personal conduct, and when she is
adjudged ready the studio will risk fifteen hundred dollars
or more on a screen test. Only a fortunate few of these kids
break through and become known, because that personality
spark is rare. Nevertheless, this department has brought
along such engaging and profitable stars as Elizabeth Tay-
lor, Lana Turner, Kathryn Grayson, June Allyson, Esther
Williams, Van Johnson, Dean Stockwell, Ava Gardner and
Janet Leigh. A manufacturing business would probably
call this their New Product Development division, and
while it is expensive it protects future earnings.

You may think this odd at first glance, but our problem
on *Next Voice* had very little to do with the fact that the
casting of recognized stars would add twenty-five percent
to the cost of the picture. Stars are a very practical form of
insurance; they protect our investment in a film, a fact
which accounts for some of the seemingly ridiculous salaries. This certainly demands a "for instance," so let's look
into our casting of Jimmy Stewart in *The Stratton Story*.

Let's say that Stewart's price for the picture was somewhere around $200,000. He would be tied up for a term

of some ten weeks, and while he would be at the studio ten hours a day for six days each week and would spend most of his evenings for two or three months studying the part, the pay check still represented a lot of money. Stewart wasn't on our contract list. Nevertheless, we were sufficiently sure of making a profit on his cost that we hired him to come to the lot.

Now then suppose we had had under contract a man named Bill Jones. Suppose he was James Stewart's identical twin in appearance, and just as good an actor. And now suppose further that he would work for nothing, absolutely free. Instead of saving that $200,000, the studio would have lost a hatful of money on the deal. That's the star system in action. Mostly you buy a ticket to a picture because you like the answer to the question, "Who's in it?" The simple placing of the name James Stewart in newspaper advertising and on theatre marquees would sell so many more tickets than the identical picture starring Bill Jones that we would recover Jim's salary and have a substantial profit left over. An economist would probably class a star as a form of natural monopoly.

A certain few critics seem convinced that the presence of a star automatically insures a banal film, while an unknown actor guarantees freshness. Of course any such generalization is silly. Unknown Vivien Leigh added freshness to *Gone With the Wind*, but Gable's presence certainly didn't hurt it artistically, and his star draw added millions of dollars to the gross. As great a property as *Father of the Bride* is greater because of Spencer Tracy. Stars and unknowns are good or bad at their craft as individuals, not by class. If I feel that the star is suited to the part and the story, I see nothing ignoble or inartistic in letting his popularity increase the number of people who see my picture.

But *Next Voice* felt as though it might be outside the standard rules. Maybe we had such a strong and novel story that we could arouse the public's want-to-see on the angle of "What's it about?" rather than "Who's in it?" We would certainly have a more believable picture. We all tend to applaud the naturalness of foreign films because the faces are unfamiliar and we therefore accept them as the true characters. In *Next Voice*, known stars would impress you as familiar people in a change of costume, whereas you'd tend to accept competent unknowns as Joe and Mary themselves. This picture could fall flat unless its audience believed it utterly. It was certainly a case where we must cast the story, not story the cast.

That night out at the house when we had dictated the story, I realized that I had been subconsciously seeing all the action in terms of one particular young actor, James Whitmore. If you were to pass Jim on the street and wonder who he was, you would guess him as an aircraft worker long before you'd think him an actor. I had seen him first on the stage in *Command Decision*. He had been noticed within the industry as the dogged, laconic top sergeant in *Battleground* (later he was nominated for the "best supporting actor" Oscar on the strength of it). Since then he had portrayed a sixty-year-old Civil War prisoner in *The Outriders* and a hunchbacked crook in *The Asphalt Jungle*. But the public had not yet hung a tag on him.

That same night after we'd finished dictating, Mrs. Schary had suggested Nancy Davis to play Mary. This idea took a bit of getting used to: this would be an exacting star role and Nancy had had only three small parts in pictures, and all of them had been on the "society" side rather than a middle-class wife and mother. But in her favor was the fact that her looks and manner and inner self were "nice" rather than cover-girl glamorous. And she was an actress by profession rather than by accident.

Incidentally, both Jim and Nancy are representative of the new generation in screen acting. Both of them set about becoming actors with the same earnest intent and preparation with which they would have embarked upon the profession of medicine or law. Jim's father is a member of the Buffalo City Planning Commission; Nancy's father is a Chicago brain surgeon and her mother was a successful actress. Jim graduated from Yale in 1942 and, after seeing action with the Marines in the South Pacific, studied in the American Theatre Wing and the Actor's Studio under the noted director Elia Kazan. Nancy majored in drama at Smith College, spent her summer vacations doing stock, and after graduation did supporting parts on the New York stage.

These are highly intelligent, well-bred young people who have approached the acting profession with the respect it deserves and intend to make it their life's work. We're getting more and more of them these days, and pictures will be the better for them.

Artistically, my heart was set on Jim for *Next Voice*, and I certainly wanted to test Nancy. But practically, I wanted some expert advice before risking a decision. Without naming the actors I was considering, I told the *Next Voice* story to several people whose judgment I valued.

When I threw the *Next Voice* story at Billy Grady, head of the Casting Department, and asked him who he'd put in the lead, he snapped back, "Jim Whitmore. You'd be crazy

to think of anybody else." Bill Wellman, who had directed
Whitmore in *Battleground* and would have to direct him in
this picture, felt the same way. So did the veteran executive
Eddie Mannix. Mr. Mayer said, and meant it, "I don't care
what the picture costs, it's a story you've got to tell. Joe
Smith should be an unfamiliar face." Equally comforting
was the vote for Whitmore from slight, unassuming talent
executive Benny Thau, whose record in terms of casting
and handling stars lends great weight to his recommendations. It was settled. Joe Smith would be Jim Whitmore.

But Nancy was still a question. Before gambling the cost
of a screen test for the part—even the greatest stars are
usually tested for each new role—Wellman and I invited
Nancy to the office to "read" for the part. I remember
coming out of the office and seeing her waiting next to Jim
on one of the straight chairs in the anteroom, her fingers
clasped tight in her lap to conceal the turbulent emotions
which her enormous brown eyes betrayed.

There was a lot at stake for her. She was on contract
with us, but that merely means money for awhile; it does
not of itself put you on the screen. Just a few weeks before,
Nancy had tested for her big chance, the feminine lead opposite Cary Grant in *Crisis*. The test was excellent. But the
producer and the director both felt that Paula Raymond
was better for the part. In a case where the men intimately
concerned feel very strongly about a point, I try to remember how I felt when an executive could twist my picture
away from my conception, and unless I'm absolutely sure
they're seriously wrong I let their decision hold. When
Nancy's hopes were dashed she was devastated, naturally
enough. I had talked to her as best I could, telling her that
this was show business and there would be more disappoint-

ments ahead, perhaps worse ones; that if her courage wasn't
strong enough to lick this disappointment it might be best
to go back home now. Her courage had been equal to that
challenge. And now here she was again. For a second I
hated my job as I realized that in a few minutes I might
have to find the words to tell her she wouldn't do.

But everybody seemed very easy and casual as we came
into the airy conference room and grouped down at one
end of the long table. We opened up the scripts and they
began reading the lines aloud. We had planned to have Jim
and Nancy read just the breakfast scene which opens the
picture and two or three assorted emotional excerpts that
come later on. But Bill and I got so absorbed in the way
these two superb young people began making the story
live and breathe that we decided not to stop them and the
reading went on uninterrupted for an hour until we came
to the words, "The End." None of us said anything for a
minute or two; we couldn't. Then Bill broke it up with (I
had been reading the other parts), "We're sorry, Schary,
but you won't do." Somebody asked what date to set the
screen test for Nancy. The question struck us funny. After
a reading like this, a test would just be a waste of everybody's time.

Fortunately for our nervous systems, the rest of the casting went along in a more routine fashion. The script had
gone to Leonard Murphy and Jimmy Broderick, one of
the teams in the downstairs casting office, and Leonard had
broken it down into a list of the several feature, minor and
bit parts which the action required, marking against each
the type and the price he would probably have to pay.

Incidentally, only the key supporting parts were to be
cast now, before the shooting started. It may seem risky to

put a picture into work with only the star and feature people actually set, but it is so difficult to forecast the exact date on which a minor player will be wanted that, to avoid conflict in the player's schedule between this job and jobs at other studios, minor parts are usually cast only a day or so ahead of the actual appearance.

If you were to be called in to be interviewed for one of these parts, you would find Leonard's quarters a tiny room near the street just big enough for his desk and two armchairs (actor and agent) not marked by Oriental splendor. Since just a few spoken lines, even a look or a single bit of business can get a laugh or make a moment that audiences remember, Leonard's memory has to be a mental card file of faces, forms, voices, mannerisms, and special aptitudes, indexed with names and salary rates. The illustrated *Players Directory* sits on his desk, of course, but he keeps his mental file constantly re-stocked by viewing most of the films produced here and abroad, including the clunkers, all of the visiting stage attractions, most of the hopeful little-theatre shows, the ice shows and all other events where talent might crop up.

For the part of young Johnny Smith, Leonard brought three boys up to the conference room and it looked as though we had hit the jackpot with the first boy interviewed. He was a nice manly youngster, and when I asked him, "What do you make of the story, Bobby?" he showed a very clear understanding. He read a couple of scenes with his "father," Jim Whitmore, including one very demanding emotional scene where he worries about his mother—"Can women die from having babies?" He did beautifully. We sent him out to the anteroom, but since the other two boys were already on hand it seemed needlessly cruel to deny them the satisfaction of having had a chance, so they were called in one by one. The second boy confirmed our opinion: he had a nice appealing quality, but he was babyish, and, as Bill expressed it, "People wouldn't believe that he would have the thoughts Johnny has." Then the third boy came in. We were polite as he started to read, then suddenly the atmosphere went tight. Wellman could barely wait until the door had closed behind the boy before he went into a rave which expressed the feelings of all of us: "Did you *see* him when he worried about his mother!" His name was Gary Gray. There was no need to ask for opinions. I told Leonard to sign the boy for the part and also see about putting him under contract to the studio, and to try to find some small parts in other pictures for the other two boys.

Leonard said, "Now you see why we never stop looking."

8

The distribution of the "okay scripts" set wheels in motion in varied departments all over the seventy-five acres. Now the heads of the key departments came together for the official kick-off, the first of a series of meetings. Called a "set meeting," it took place in the sunny high-ceilinged office of art director Cedric Gibbons.

The word "art" is really a misnomer. An art director in films is much more than a lovely person in charge of color schemes; he is a sort of dramatic engineering designer. Basically, the job of Japanese-American Eddie Imazu, the associate art director to whom Gibbons assigned direct responsibility for *Next Voice*, is to design the sets. But many scenes are not shot on stage sets, and still they must be planned by somebody. And the designer cannot even begin to lay out the walls of his stage sets until he knows exactly what dramatic action those walls must permit, and from what camera angles the action will be shot. And since problems like these must often be worked out long before a director checks in on a picture, Art is really the "How-to-do-it" department.

Eddie was assigned to the project on January 23rd. In the days before the "set meeting" he got together his "set breakdown," going through the script scene by scene and making notations of all locales mentioned and the number of scenes to be played in each. Beside each locale he had listed his preliminary recommendation as to whether we should construct a set for it inside a sound stage, shoot it on an off-the-lot location with existing scenery and buildings, use outdoor buildings on the studio's own back lot, resort to miniature work, stock shots, rear-projection "process," Newcombe process, or any one of several combinations thereof which I'll describe later. With location man Charlie Coleman and a still cameraman, he had scouted various locations for certain sequences, and then taken Wellman out to view the locations which looked best in the stills.

At the meeting, Eddie turned in some very rough sketches of the stage sets which would have to be provided to mount the film script as it now stood, plus a preliminary set budget. At this point, it looked as though the story would need about forty sets, none very elaborate and twelve of them either on location or on the back lot, at a cost of around $35,000 for design and construction.

Even on a big glamour musical, the designer starts thinking about his sets in terms of their "spirit" long before he creates their actual appearance. On *Next Voice* the spirit of the sets would help tell the story. The house tells us what kind of people Joe and Mary are before we even see them. The mood of the two cocktail bar sets is particularly vital to the mood of the scenes they enclose, for bar number one is smart and sleek, making logical Joe's temptation, and bar number two, making natural his repentance and shame, is subtly dingy and sordid. Later Eddie's draftsman, himself an architect by training, would take the scratch-pad designs and run them out into construction blueprints, inching through the vast catalogs of stock units in storage from past pictures to see what existing material he could utilize.

Joe's two-bedroom house would have to be all new construction, because it must match the existing dwelling

which had been chosen for the outdoor location. But both
of the bar sets could use stock, if shuffled about in a new
arrangement and given flair with a little new work. The
hospital corridor could be moved in from a scene dock
and reassembled practically intact, with a saving of several
thousand dollars over all-new construction and no loss of
pictorial effect. Often Eddie will have a sketch artist paint
color visualizations of the sets for the director, and sometimes where physical action is involved he will have an
artist develop a series of continuity sketches, like comic-
strips. But Wellman can visualize blueprints for himself and
has clear ideas of exactly how he is going to play the action.

Eddie's efforts crystallized in the form of blueprints for
the construction department, where skilled prop makers
began bringing them to life in the form of tabletop model
sets.

For Jack Dawn, one-time film cowboy who introduced
sculptor's methods to makeup (many wounded veterans
thank Jack for the cleverly fitted "skin-pieces" which conceal their disfigurements) *Next Voice* would be a walk-
through; there was nothing in it like the leprechauns in
Three Wise Fools whose great ears must flap on cue. Jack
is accustomed to challenges such as that of the director who
demanded a hitherto unheard-of effect in a Gene Lockhart
scene—as Gene lay unconscious amid flames, the audience
must see a blister actually rising on his cheek.

It was a make-up apprentice who came up with the solu-
tion for that one: he mashed an Alka Seltzer tablet into
powder, sealed the powder under a thin rubber blister
cemented to Gene's cheek, and then injected water at

the proper moment with a hypodermic needle. Audiences screamed.

Dawn's guiding principle is that all make-up must seem like no make-up, and our desire for absolute realism in *Next Voice* resulted in the decision to use no make-up at all on anybody, not even the stars. Hair stylist Sydney Guilaroff gave Nancy a simple bob which, like Mary Smith, she would wash and set herself, and, except for Nancy's normal lipstick, that was that.

Three different people in Sam Kress' camphor-smelling domain broke the *Next Voice* script down into "wardrobe plots," in which each costume to be worn by each player became known as a "change" and christened with a number. Costumes, of course, must do much more than merely glamorize the physical attributes of the actors. The suntans and Marine windbreaker which Jim would wear at the Aircraft plant would build out the audience's knowledge of his character—one more veteran using up his Service clothes —and the slightly ill-fitting blue serge suit made him obviously the kind of a fellow who owned one good suit and wore it to church and lodge meeting.

Wardrobe man Bob Streeter would select the "character" clothes for Jim and the other men in the cast from the vast stock in the fourteen wardrobe rooms scattered over the three lots. Male actors are expected to supply their own "modern" clothes, unless a scene involves a risk of spilling, burning or other damage—in which event we protect against damage by making several "doubles" of the costume—or if the director demands something special which the actor would not ordinarily own. Streeter had to buy

Jim's Sunday blue suit, and after it was altered (with expert inexpertness) he sent it to the laundry and then did some sandpapering to age it, and had Jim wear it around the lot a few days.

Rhea Meunier and stylist Ida Loewen were accumulating the women's wardrobe in much the same manner, and the costumes were gradually being built into "lines." Each change, from head to foot, including all visible accessories, would be kept together on a hanger as a numbered unit, and strung along a bar set aside for each player.

The wardrobe people' can turn up such items as three-legged trousers, Roman armor or a Coronation gown without the lift of an eyebrow, but they gulped once or twice before they swallowed one *Next Voice* problem. Probably never had a movie shown, in scene after scene, a leading lady whom the plot required to be only a week away from her baby's birth. The result was a selection of three carefully fitted pads of varying prominence, and one of the odder studio sights must have been Wellman, father of six, and I, father of three, arguing like a pair of hens in this new Battle of the Bulge. Over this unusual foundation the fitters built Nancy's simple wardrobe.

Standard procedure might have been to have Nancy's clothes created by one of the famous designers, such as Helen Rose, whose work adds markedly to the allure of period, musical and glamour pictures. But we checked Nancy's costuming garment by garment to protect the realistic atmosphere we had in mind, and Ida Loewen bought every piece of Nancy's wardrobe in local stores at the $12.95 sort of price which Mary Smith would have paid. She did, however, add an occasional bit of embroidery or a bow, such as a Mary with good taste would have done, and of course all the clothes were fitted with the usual extraordinary care. Each tiny frame of film is magnified up to sixty thousand times when it appears on the screen, and the slightest imperfection in the fitting would billow out to make Nancy look messy on the screen as Mary Smith would never have looked in life. The camera and projector combine to make a merciless lie detector.

It was about this time that the stars had their first actual working contact with the picture. They came to Wardrobe for final fittings, and reported to Stage 2 for camera tests on the costuming. One purpose of the tests was to check our handling of the pregnancy problem with the Breen Office. But equally important was to find out what the camera and projector thought of our judgment, and, as always, the tests proved their worth: a checkered blouse proved so "busy" that it would have stolen any scene in which it appeared, and a robe moved in such an odd way that it made Nancy seem to be hopping as she walked.

While all this was going on, the merchandising side of the studio organization was also coming up to speed. The best picture in the world is of no effect unless a lot of people see it, and people will come to see it only if they know about it. Therefore, as soon as his staff had had time to read the script, Howard Strickling brought his publicity and exploitation people over to the office for the setup meeting. I thought as I looked around the table how disappointed a cartoonist might be, for all of these "press agents" were quiet, competent people without a plaid suit in the lot, here simply because they were experts at reporting, and planting items with the press, art, or advertising.

Since the competition of many good films for the movie-

goers' attention is too rugged to let us depend on the "better mousetrap" theory of merchandising, it is the job of
these men to so gather and disseminate information about
each picture that it achieves maximum "penetration"—
which simply means that as many people as possible are
made conscious of the title and stars—and then expand this
penetration into a maximum want-to-see.

The assembly settled into quick agreement on two
points: *Next Voice* might turn out to be a very good picture, but it would certainly be very tough to sell. There
were none of the standard "handles" on the picture; no famous stars, no spectacle, no sex draw, no high action, no
glamorous sets or musical numbers or clothes—and the
story nub of God speaking to people on the radio was one
which good taste would forbid our using in advertising.
Good taste would also forbid our resorting to the stock
approaches or distorted selling angles such as, "Who was
the woman who came into his life as the world rocked"
in a "searing drama of a man's temptation and a woman's
desperation." The picture would have to be presented to
the public straightforwardly for exactly what it was.

With that challenge the ideas began to flow, ideas for
magazine articles, art layouts in the picture magazines,
advertising slogan lines, exploitation gadgets such as card-
board phonograph records, and so on far into the afternoon. But at the end it still looked as though we might find
ourselves testing the old better-mousetrap theory before
we got through, which would put it squarely up to director Wellman.

Jim Merrick, a deft young Englishman who had worked
comfortably with publicity-shunning Wellman on *Battleground*, was assigned as the "unit man" on *Next Voice*.

He kept in touch with Bill, the stars and the various departments to garner items of news about the picture which the planters could feed the trade papers. And he spent a good deal of time in his room on the third floor of the white-columned Publicity Building laying out his "still plot" of plantable pictures which the still photographer should pick up during production, and writing his *Campaign Book*. This would outline possible stories, art layouts, radio tie-ins and other exploitation devices to be "sold" to the four hundred thirty-five accredited columnists, fan-magazine writers, and other outlets. Whose co-operation, we hoped, would help make the public curious about those five words—five words on whose fate would rest the studio's investment and the hopes of many people, *The Next Voice You Hear*.

9

Efficiency experts trained in other industries are usually baffled when they try to fit the making of a movie to their standard rules. The fact is, a movie is essentially a handcraft operation, a one-of-a-kind custom job—but it must be made on a factory basis, with production-line economies, if we're to hold the price down within reach of most of the people. The job is to do this without losing the picture's individuality.

The economic pressures are very great. Some pictures succumb to the system and emerge as factory products. Other pictures come off the line vital and fresh, their individuality unimpaired. The difference lies in the creators. As with books, paintings or plays, all the films can't be good; there aren't enough good creators. But the intentions are good: nobody in Hollywood ever started out with the *intention* of making a bad picture. Within the limits of his circumstances and abilities he did the best he could.

A business theorist would probably chart the picture-making process in terms of two teams. The custom side of the picture is developed by the creative team—the producer, writer, director, actors, cameraman and art director. Those manufacturing operations which are more or less the same for all pictures—construction, set operation, company management, etc.—make up the duties of the Production Department.

The Production Department has full responsibility for

the physical progress and cost of the picture from the time the final script is okayed. Cost hounds, expediters, anglers, worriers, valiant warriors for the sacred schedule, Jo Cohn's young men are often met by the query, "Do you want it good or do you want it Tuesday?" and are the apocryphal authors of the classic reply, "A tree is a tree and a rock is a rock, shoot it in Griffith Park."

Production's direct representative on the *Next Voice* company would be Ruby Rosenberg, the Unit Manager. Now, in the two-story white wooden barracks which houses the Department, he had finished his Sequence Breakdown and was trying to put together that series of compromises known as the Shooting Schedule. And while the Schedule might not make particularly romantic reading, it would be the key to success or failure of the whole enterprise as an economic unit of production.

Not everybody realizes that the cost of a movie is not primarily made up of physical items such as sets and costumes, nor even less tangible charges such as story cost and script preparation. The prime cost of a motion picture is *time*—time in production, from the start of photography to its finish. The British call it "days on the floor." True, several expensive people draw salaries during the preparatory period of a picture, but there are only a few of them and they are using only office rooms and other inexpensive facilities. And while there is still important work to be done after photography is finished, again the number of people involved and the facilities are comparatively inexpensive. Lately you may have seen references in the news to shortened shooting schedules. That is because the *number of days in production* controls the really heavy cost items such as actors' salaries, wages and salaries for the large

stage and technical crews, and a very considerable charge
for overhead.

The word "overhead" has come to be a bad word, but
overhead expense is a natural and inescapable part of any
operation where one man plans the work of others and
where the work involves any use of property. Take our
Wardrobe Department, for example: we could charge *Next
Voice* directly with the outright cost of the costumes we
buy especially for the film, and salaries for the wardrobe
man and woman who actually "work" the picture. But the
picture must somehow also pay its share of maintaining the
studio's stock of costumes, owning the buildings in which
they are stored, and compensate Sam Kress and others for
their management work. That, and a share of similar costs
for other departments whose work helps make the picture,
goes into overhead.

At M-G-M overhead also includes such direct picture
costs as stage rentals (an independent producer would have
paid a rental lot at least two thousand dollars a day for the
stages tied up by *Next Voice*). It includes the electric current for the lighting (a single set for an Esther Williams
Technicolor picture may use more current than a city the
size of Tacoma). Such service departments as Legal Research, International, Censorship, Casting and Library are
paid for by overhead, as well as the use of vital back-lot
facilities such as the Sign Shop and Gun Room, and general
studio services such as trucking and messengers and hospital personnel. And finally it must include the indirect overhead chargeable to any business operation such as interest,
insurance, taxes, pension provisions, research, inventory
write-offs, and compensation for executive management.
Incidentally, all of the studios have made substantial re-

ductions in their overhead load in the last two or three years, and the situation is healthier than it has been for a long time.

Despite the economy, however, visitors to the stages always go away shaking their heads over the apparent lavishness, particularly at the large number of people who seem to be just standing about. Again, much of this is tied to the high cost per shooting day of a company. Take the hypothetical case of a dental specialist who might be kept on the set to fix young Gary Gray's lost baby tooth and who can send him back to work an hour earlier than had we had to send the boy to a dentist off the lot. If the stand-by dentist performed only that one brief job for a whole month's pay, the saved hour of shooting time could have shown the studio a profit of several hundred percent on his salary.

The Next Voice company would not be nearly as expensive as some, but it could easily run to fifteen thousand dollars per day, and even more on an outside location day with a heavy list of extras. If for some reason such as bad weather, the illness of a star, or whatever, shooting had to be suspended, much of that cost would go right on. And so in planning his shooting schedule, Rosenberg knew that once the cameras began to turn it would be his responsibility to see that nothing stopped production or slowed it down. Everything and everybody must be ready when needed and no alibis would be accepted.

The *Next Voice* happened to be divided into 172 scenes. But a shooting script which would reach the screen in exactly the same length might contain up to 500 scene numbers, if the writer and producer felt it necessary to write out each camera angle in advance. But most directors justifiably consider the handling of the camera as in their

province, and Bill Wellman's manipulation of the action
would be far more effective than what we might suggest.
Also, working so intimately with Bill on *Battleground* had
given me a good notion of the way he would break up his
scenes, and had reassured me that he didn't go in for a lot
of needless setups. So our screenplay was written in a comparatively small number of master scenes in which the action ran uninterrupted for as long as five or six pages. When
Ruby Rosenberg made his initial breakdown, he grouped
the scenes into eighty short sequences, each sequence link-
ing a series of scenes which occurred in one set in one more
or less continuous progression.

Now Ruby began to work out his shooting schedule by
putting these eighty sequences "on the board." To each
sequence he allotted a long narrow celluloid strip which
he coded with letters or numbers in appropriate squares to
indicate the set, the season, whether day or night, interior
or exterior, reminders of any special music, sound, special
effects (rain), vehicles, animals, props and any special reminders. He finished by noting which actors would work
in the sequence, the number of pages of script represented,
and an estimate of how many days or fractional days the
sequence would require for shooting. When these strips
were laid side by side in a slotted board, all the jigsaw
pieces which made up the total production puzzle stood
out clearly in a sort of visible index.

As Ruby sorted these strips around in endless trial combinations, it became clear why the scenes of a movie are
usually shot "out of continuity," a process which results
in such incongruities as Mary having her baby several days
before she is photographed hurrying to the hospital. Moving the company from one set to another, which involves

relighting, and particularly moving from one building to another uses up time and hence costs money.

Therefore, in theory, Ruby would like to shoot all the sequences occurring in any given set in one continuous session. But this is extreme and seldom comes to pass, because directors know that actors cannot catch the real spirit of scenes which are shot ridiculously far out of continuity.

On the other hand, screen actors draw their pay from the first day they work to the last, even though they may be idle several days in between. So Ruby shuffled his celluloid strips back and forth to compress the engagement of the more expensive supporting actors into the shortest practical compass of days from call to dismissal.

A lot of other considerations affected the grouping. Our boy, Gary, would have to go to school a certain number of hours each day, and each day's agenda must therefore include some scenes in which he would not appear. The locker room and cocktail bar sets were ordered to be built a few days ahead of schedule, so we could switch to them if Gary or Nancy got sick. Our off-lot location day at a school had to be set for the February 22nd holiday, rain or shine. ("Let it rain," said Wellman; "real kids go to school in the rain.") The Douglas Aircraft location had to be fixed for Saturday, the 25th, when most of the plant would be cleared for the holiday and two beautiful bombers would hit the head of the assembly line side by side and make a wonderful background. If we tried to shoot the average picture in its strict story continuity, we'd have to charge you twice as much for your ticket. And you wouldn't come to our show.

Shooting schedules for feature-length pictures vary all the way from seven or eight days for the quickies to two

and three months, sometimes more, for the epics. Back in
the plush days, important pictures were figured to use one
shooting day for each minute of screen footage. Since the
shrinkage in foreign grosses and other factors started the
economy wave, all studios have shortened the schedules of
all pictures, which is healthy, but a schedule of thirty to
thirty-five days for a quality dramatic picture is still considered fast shooting. However, even that schedule would
be too long for the money we could afford to invest in the
uncertain *Next Voice*. Ruby crossed his fingers and mimeographed a schedule which called for twenty-two shooting
days.

Wellman scanned the schedule with that skeptical blue
eye and nodded grimly, "I'll make it." The Production fellows figured they'd probably get licked, but it would be a
big thing in town if they got away with it. And I felt se-
cretly that if the twenty-two days stretched to twenty-
four or five, it would be all right with me.

Production's representative on the set is the Assistant
Director, recognizable by the harassed and preoccupied
expression which comes from trying continually to keep
three moves ahead of his director. Ours was a slim, black-
haired young man named Joel Freeman who had started
with M-G-M as a messenger and come up through the
more or less standard route of production-office clerk,
company script clerk, and second assistant director. This
would be his initial job as a "first." The short shooting
schedule would put a stiff responsibility on him, but we
figured that his ambition to make good on the opportunity
would supply the drive to keep him alert and jumping during those three weeks of fifteen-hour days.

The title of Assistant Director does not describe his job too well nowadays. He has come to be more of an arranger and expediter: his primary responsibility is to make sure that everything and everybody needed during the production will be on hand in the right place at the right time and in the proper condition. It was a "first" who thought of throwing the box lunch sandwiches on the water off Catalina when a famous director demanded sea gulls in his shot, and who, when the gulls swooped down in a beautiful line from left to right, was typically rewarded with, "We're losing 'em against the sails. Send 'em in the other way!"

However, the assistant does have the directorial responsibility of arranging background and atmospheric action. In *Next Voice* when you see Joe Smith and his friends coming out of the bowling alley, you'll see a couple of passers-by walk in. It was Joel's job to decide from the script that this secondary action was necessary to add validity to the scene, and to requisition the extras. When the scene was shot he cued them in at the proper moment.

This background function can become quite complex, and it did later on in one sequence where, on a Saturday afternoon in the plot, Joe walked across the park from his house to Mr. Brannan's. Joel worked up unobtrusive action to background Joe all the way across, from ball-playing to car washing to the Good Humor wagon with crowding kids. Joel's script breakdown listed our probable requirements of bit players and extras in each scene, and this data went, along with Rosenberg's schedule, to the Estimating Department.

Another kind of estimate had already been made in a script-lined upstairs cubbyhole by Lauren Amell and Honore Janney. They are footage estimators; and they "time out" each script to figure how many minutes the finished movie will play on the screen.

Every picture has a certain running length which is right for its particular set of values and appeals. I think we ought to determine that length fairly closely in the preparatory stage rather than in the preview theatre, and then shoot just about the footage we'll actually use in the release. If a story comes along that I think will hold up for three hours on the screen, I'll fight to make it in that length. But often there's a tendency to allot a picture more time than its audience will think it's worth. To some extent I'm voicing a personal phobia here; I feel that most of us are apt to tell a story or a joke at too much length, so that it begins to drag, and I'm always trying to see where we can cut pictures without loss. Each picture is its own problem. *Gone With the Wind* didn't have a wasted foot of film, for me. But I've seen one-hour pictures that were sixty minutes too long.

Commercially, particularly in these days of high costs and double features, only a very occasional sure-smash epic like *Annie Get Your Gun* can command a running time of more than ninety minutes, but plenty of lesser pictures have gone all the way to preview at two hours or more, and not merely in the dear dead past. I expect any picture to be trimmed a few minutes in cutting, if only for pace. But since it may be cheaper by several hundred thousands of dollars to throw away thirty pages of script than thirty minutes of expensively filmed drama, these pre-shooting footage estimates make very useful reading.

Amell and Mrs. Janney work independently, "playing" the picture in their minds scene by scene against the stop watch, then checking their results against each other. They know from long experience the tempos and ways of working of most of our directors and stars, and they can pretty well gauge the pace at which the film will move. "With Wallace Beery," Amell remembers, "you'd have to figure time for him to hitch up his pants and spit before a speech."

You might expect that musical numbers and dance routines would be impossible to estimate in advance, since they're seldom worked out in detail much before shooting, but Amell's simple approach is, "How long could I sit still for this routine in a theatre?" He finds that he tends to get the twitches long before many writers. The estimate on the *Next Voice* script was 7,685 feet, which would run just about eighty-five minutes. After the picture had gone through all the changes, and shooting had been completed and the first editing done, the footage of the "first cut" ran 7,630 feet. The estimators had missed the boat by almost forty seconds.

One by one the fiscal forecasts resulting from the various departmental breakdowns channeled over into the pine-paneled room in the Production Building where Joe Finn and his assistants were working out the final budget on the picture. Physically, the budget would emerge about the shape of a *Saturday Evening Post* or *Collier's*, but any fiction it contained would be strictly unintentional. Thirty-seven main cost elements were listed on the summary sheet, ending with the item which Joe considers his personal enemy, Miscellaneous. The word had gone around that this picture was to be a test case, and the departments had taken it as a challenge: everybody had used their heads to save their wallets, and the final figure was very encouraging.

Nevertheless, the erasers were in plain sight at the second
of the major conferences, the Budget Meeting in the office
of Production Manager Walter Strohm. He served as chair-
man, with watchdog Jo Cohn flanking him, and sitting
on the leather couches or propped back in straight chairs
against the wall were the representatives of the major controllable budget items—sets, casting, wardrobe—and the
men who would make the picture, Bill Wellman, his cameraman Bill Mellor, and their assistants.

In the middle of the budget was an eleven-page section
which highlighted these controllable expense items. Each
sequence was listed, with its set, estimated shooting time,
the number of bits and extras and the prices Leonard Murphy expected to pay them. Walter took these up one by
one, and the sound of hatchets was heard in the land. Could
this set be eliminated and the action played in another?
Could this scene be played at night so we could kill some
of the expensive detail on the set and eliminate a painted
backing? Did we need sixty kids in the school exterior or
could Wellman angle his action to get his effect with less?
Do we need so many different radio announcers, or could
the family always listen to one or two favorites? We've
figured $200 for the doctor bit in the hospital, haven't we
anyone in stock? Since we don't actually use the bowling
alley attached to the cocktail bar, can't we just suggest
it with shadows and sound? In the montage where Joe is
looking for runaway Johnny, the cutter won't use all eight
spots listed, so why shoot them? Let's kill the gas station,
which we'd have to build, and pick up the standing theatre
foyer on Lot 2 some night when we're working over there
anyway. . . .

Refreshingly, these meetings show some accent on adding budget as well as slashing it, when the additions may pay off on the screen. In the locker-room scene, goes the talk, hadn't we better boost the estimated prices for the bit voices; we'll need good character men, not just extras . . . better use a stunt driver for Joe's "near miss"—don't take any chances, use stunt drivers in both cars.

As is inevitable when creative minds focus on the bits and pieces of a screenplay, new ideas crop up to improve the picture. Let's use well-known radio announcers, some-one suggests, they'll add a plus. . . . There's no value in just a guy walking through the background, make him a letter-carrier . . . a couple of those school kids ought to be Negroes, but let's just take them for granted in the crowd and don't feature them. . . . And how about hav-ing some of the kids dressed in those cowboy outfits? "What are all these background people going to be doing in the second saloon?" asked Wellman. "Take them out; now that God's on the radio nobody's going to the saloons and there's just this one girl sitting at the long shadowy bar, it'll be a wonderful lonesome feeling." When the meeting broke up it looked like a standoff; we'd added about as much money as we had taken out, but the picture had come a few steps upward and the plans were more crystallized in everybody's mind.

It isn't giving away any secret to jump ahead a few months and admit that *Next Voice* was brought in at a very satisfactory over-all cost figure. But it should also be ad-mitted that on this particular film certain essential charges which would loom large on most cost sheets were either absent entirely or ridiculously low, and they could have boosted our cost by $250,000 or more. We paid no big stars' fees, and stories which can attract people to theatres without stars are not plentiful enough to fill any studio's production program. Since I draw my own salary for executive duties, this picture did not have to pay a producer's fee, and there was a lesser saving on the writing budget.

But these latter savings can be repeated in many circumstances: in fact, M-G-M and other studios are going in more and more heavily for double-duty deals where one qualified man acts as a writer-producer, writer-director, or perhaps all three. Moreover, all studios have made substantial cuts in their overhead personnel; all have shifted many contract people over to a free-lance basis where they are paid only when working. We are being tougher about our story buys, taking on only those stories which we know in advance how we'll make, and thus reducing our abandonment rate. By turning out more features per year with the same facilities and contract people, we are dividing our overhead into more units and putting less of an overhead burden on each picture.

Economy involves a lot more than merely firing people. In fact, one of our most promising aspects is the plan on which Studio Manager Bill Spencer is working to smooth out this notorious feast-or-famine operation into a reasonably continuous flow of work, whereby we hope to have five pictures in production as a steady thing and thus provide a reasonably constant income to a solid core of our people.

I have a strong belief, and the *Next Voice* cost sheet bears it out, that the three lines of attack which are going to bring our soaring costs under control are these: Clear, direct, straight thinking; creative discipline; and exhaustive pre-production preparation of every picture. Of course, all three can sing their heads off and never be heard unless they're backed with talent. And the most exhaustive preparation of a production is not much good if it's done by rote, dutifully—there has to be a real enthusiasm on the lot. On *Next Voice*, all these factors worked together. It's unfair to single out any one, but perhaps the most informative was the pre-production woodshedding through which Bill Wellman put the project.

10

Bill Wellman is a turbulent character in suntan pants and a windbreaker, with rumpled gray hair, the unselfconsciousness of a four-year-old child, and a charm that reaches out and grabs you by the heart. His lean face manages to be both boyish and satanic at the same time; he has a husky voice, a cowboy's walk, a headlong directness, a terrible memory for names, a dislike of being indoors, a fabulous history, and a complete knowledge of how to make pictures.

A sure way to embarrass Bill is to start talking about his hits. At the first mention of *Wings, Nothing Sacred* or *A Star Is Born,* Billy will squirm and switch the conversation to one of his flops. He says the only profit for a director lies in "figuring out why I loused something up."

A famous member of the craft once described the director's function as "realizing on the screen all the values inherent in the script." Billy does this on the run, keeps right on driving and comes out with a picture nine feet tall.

The script told the Story of *The Next Voice* in words. Bill would have to tell it through a lens, with visual images on a screen. Although a script is usually complete as to dialogue, the writer would stack up a clutter of pages ceiling high if he attempted to describe in detail all the actions and reactions of the scenes, the light and shade, the nuances of attitudes, the bits of "business," all that goes into giving his characters the stuff of life that will make those characters into people. And while these things will exist in a good script by suggestion or implication, their accomplishment in screen terms is a province of the director.

Every single one of the ideas and bits and details which give sparkle to a picture has to be thought of by somebody. You can think of them on the set during production with the crew standing idle and the overhead ticking like a platinum taxi meter. Or you can think of them ahead of time, shooting the picture in your mind before you turn a crank, and meet most of the emergencies before they happen. Of course, some of the best things in the picture will be born on the set, in the heat of action, when the director actually sees and hears his live people working in and out of real walls and props and furnishings. Those improvements are usually worth all the time they take and a lot more; they make a better picture and a better picture sells more tickets. But the point is, on-set delays should be reserved for improvements, not to fill holes or repair errors which should have been uncovered in a dry run.

Bill had studied the *Next Voice* story in his office and at home, and had thought about it and talked about it until the film had already begun to exist in his mind, cut by cut. The routine preparation was already under way: Imazu, Freeman, Rosenberg and the others were continually in and out of Bill's office on the business of checking sets, approving wardrobe, selecting locations, assigning personnel, and so on. But not until very recently has it been at all common practice to let the actors in on our secret, to hold cast rehearsals before actually going on stage.

I had experimented with pre-production cast readings and rehearsals while I was at RKO. It seemed only sensible that the directors and actors should work out their funda-

mental understandings before their deliberations involved
the overhead of an expensive crew. Bill had used the
advance-rehearsal technique with considerable success on
Battleground, so we decided to repeat it here.

Wellman's office is a sunny third-floor corner in the
modernistic Directors' Building, in the middle of the production lot. Jim Whitmore was there in the khaki pants and
plaid shirt he was breaking in for the locker-room scenes;
Nancy was there with her shoes off as is her habit; Bill was
behind his desk slipping his horn-rimmed glasses on and off
as he peered at the script, and he was flanked by sunburnt
cameraman Bill Mellor and assistant director Joel Freeman.

On the wall beside Wellman's desk was an enlarged floor
plan of Joe Smith's house set in which most of the action
would take place. Clearly marked on it were the positions
of all windows, important articles of furniture, the doors
and which way they opened, and "wild" walls which could
be quickly removed to permit a switch in camera angle. Art
directors usually figure on two wild walls for each room,
but Bill usually ends up with four.

In form, these rehearsals were merely a sort of extended
"reading," with frequent breaks for comments, queries,
reminders and discussions. It was not merely a rehearsal
for the two actors. Wellman and Mellor were working out
their own jobs in terms of specific setups and action and
camera moves, and Joel Freeman was unearthing many
items which would have to be arranged for as the production progressed.

Out of the reading came a number of script changes.
Some were merely changes in dialogue lines which lay
poorly on the actor's tongue or could be improved or
dropped. Originally when Mary came home from the

hospital after the false labor young Johnny was to ask, "Where's the baby?" But Bill thought the boy would be old enough to know the essential facts of life and he feared the original line might get an unwanted audience laugh, so now Johnny would simply look at his mother and she would quietly say, "There's been a slight change of plans, Johnny. . . ." A speech of Mr. Brannan's referred to "Proverbs 6, VI" and Bill had Joel check with a minister to see into exactly what words a man like Brannan would translate those numerals. Often in a script a character's attitude has to be indicated by a speech. Now the unnecessary talk could be killed and replaced by the more probable glance or significant pantomime.

Even though the script had been worked over until it was in pretty tight shape, some of these changes were really important. Originally, when Mary was at the hospital with her false labor, Joe had gone in from the corridor to a semi-private room where two other women were helping her pack. They came out and down the corridor for Mary's line, "I feel like such a fool, leaving here as big as when I came in," and then went to the lobby for the business of paying the bill. These scenes wouldn't "come up" in rehearsal, wouldn't play with the simple, alive straightforwardness of the scenes up to that point. The upshot was that we killed the scenes in the room and the lobby, and had Mary speak her two lines of apology when she came out of a door with her suitcase into the corridor to join Joe. Not only was the new action much more clean and dramatic—Ruby cut three-quarters of a day out of his shooting schedule, Joel dropped two extras and the receptionist bit from his cast list, and Eddie Imazu canceled one $600 and one $1200 set.

As expected, the rehearsals uncovered a lot of bridges which could be crossed more cheaply before we came to them. "This business where the cop stops Joe at night," queried Wellman, "can we shoot it on the back lot, have we got a good street that fits the action? . . . We'll want all the kids to start running at once. Joel, arrange for somebody to ring the school bell for a cue. . . . Rembrandt"—meaning Mellor—"how about a long shot of the boy walking away from the car and getting lost in the crowd of youngsters going into the school? . . . This insert where Joe's foot steps gingerly on the starter pedal, pick it up when we're working on the process stage with the split-up car."

And then there was the big rainstorm, when God's voice on the radio said, "Must I send another forty days and nights of rain," and a few moments later rain would begin to fall, motivating the first real fear. At first thought you might group Joe, Mary and the boy in a tight three-shot near the radio, and background them with a window against which the raindrops would be seen. Bill knew in advance that the effect would not come off. The whole grouping would look contrived rather than natural; he would have to force a way of pulling the lace curtain away from the window, and he would not be able to move his camera sufficiently close to the glass to see the raindrops without being obvious and, worse, losing the all-important emotional reaction of the characters. Had that kind of problem waited for settlement until we were on set, either a great deal of expensive time would have been wasted, or we would have settled quickly for a bad compromise and lost a tremendously affecting moment of the picture.

The mimeographed pages of Bill's script were filling up

with scrawled notations; reminders of opportunities, pitfalls, attitudes, and bits of business. Bill is one of the great
directors of the industry, but has never gotten the public
recognition which his work deserves. I think these scrawls
explain why. Many of the bits of business with which director Ernst Lubitsch fleshed his wonderful pictures were
noticeable; they stood out in bas-relief from the planes of
the story as distinctive twists of action, recognizable as the
"Lubitsch touch." Many of Wellman's touches are equally
great, I think, but they are almost invariably bits of character action or reaction so natural and logical that they
become indigenous to the character. They're so blended
into the pattern of the whole that the audience tends to feel
them rather than give them conscious notice, with the result that the approval goes to the picture as a whole or,
when an occasional bit does catch notice, to the actor in
whose characterization it is displayed. Bill must know this,
but he keeps on throwing the business to his actors and
turning out consistently great pictures.

As I've said, these bits are natural. They're warm, and
they "tell" a character in action rather than words, but you
have to know a good deal about pictures and something
about art to realize the true bigness of these seemingly triv-
ial things. For example, Bill needed some intimate action
between Joe and Mary to put a warm personal feeling on
the finish of the picture. Every married couple probably
has some insignificant gesture that is meaningful only to
themselves, so here it would be a way that Joe has of tick-
ling Mary's ear and to which she would respond. Bill uses
it three times to build the intimacy between Joe and Mary,
reverses it once (when Mary pulls away instead of re-
sponding, we're told more dramatically than in words that

there's trouble), and at the end when Mary is wheeled out
of the delivery room, her unconscious response supplies
the emotional climax of the film.

Joe's car trouble when he left for work on the morning
of the first day would be funny, and of course his leaving
on the second day must top it. Out of that need came the
marvelous bit of pantomime where young Johnny sits at
the breakfast table and, in ridiculous synchronization with
the sounds floating in from the unseen garage, mimics the
troubles which we know off-scene Joe is undergoing in
starting his engine. In another instance, toward the end of
the picture Joe wants to say grace at dinner. Suddenly we
know a lot more about Joe and Mary from the simple fact
that Joe stumbles momentarily in the blessing, and Mary
is able to prompt him.

Some of the inventions were purely mechanical. A moment of intimacy between husband and wife wouldn't play
while Johnny was in the scene, so Bill cleared the deck and
got a free laugh by having Joe send the boy to the window
to keep watch for gabby Aunt Ethel. Other bits were mechanical, but had a spiritual result. Of the scene after Brannan's workshop where Johnny comes to understand his
father's being afraid, Bill said, "The boy must be older
than his father here," and he staged the position of the two
actors so that Joe is lower than his son, looking up.

Of course it's essential that actors come on set with their
lines memorized, but that is a matter of professional mechanics. Out of these pre-production rehearsals Jim and
Nancy learned more than the lines, more than even the inner meaning of the lines, they got an understanding of
who they were and why they did the actions in the play,
and how they felt about things. They had to learn to as-

sume their new personalities. As Jim Whitmore, a blown-out tire might mean only an inconvenience—as Joe Smith, the blowout would be a dismaying sound, a signal of a real financial blow that Joe would hate to have to tell Mary about. And as a result of going back and forth through the script, reading with Wellman and broadening their comprehension as they heard his comments, they finally got that invaluable insight, the feeling of the whole.

Nancy was spending much of her time away from the studio with a close friend of hers who was soon going to have a baby, noting every characteristic movement and emotion. The set of the Joe Smith home on Stage 18 was completed a few days ahead of production, and Jim and Nancy moved in to do their rehearsing in the actual surroundings. "This way it gets to be my own house," said Jim. "Now I can get up out of a chair and swing toward a door without having to sneak a look at where I'm going."

By Monday, February 20, the preparatory activities all over the studio were hitting their peak. On Stage 18, set decorator Ralph Hurst was putting the final lived-in touches on the living-room set, and I grinned as I saw him put a burned-out light bulb in the bowl on the buffet. I'd never thought of it before, but there must be one in every home in America.

In the locker-room set adjacent, painters were brushing the wooden I-beams into the appearance of steel; another painter was "dirtying" the big washstand, and a plumber was busily damaging a practical pipe so that the water would come out in the "trickle" which would justify Freddie Dibson's complaint. Greensmen were laying lawn and installing shrubbery on the floor around the front of the

Smith house, carpenters were stringing out the pre-fabri-
cated units for the cocktail-bar set. Out front, Joel was
checking the instant-starting gadget which Joe would pull
when he lifted the hood on his beat-up 1937 Plymouth. The
wardrobe lines were filling up; Ruby Rosenberg was sending his first call sheet to Mimeo. Even the older hands had
that tight feeling you always seem to get just before the
kickoff. Up in my office we held the final reading.

The night before, I had gone over the whole script once
again looking for spots we could improve. I wanted to expand the radio speaker's announcement in the church on
the last night, to try to get a feeling of universal brother-
hood, a feeling that all over the world all kinds of people
were doing exactly the same thing at the same instant, listening to the Voice of their Creator. Bill bought it and
made a note to take advantage of the extra footage for
a succession of cutaway bits of character business, quick
flashes of interesting people ending with Joe and Mary.
We made a final decision on separating our sequences with
the old-fashioned title-cards, *The First Day*, and so on, the
lettering to be superimposed over the most beautiful cloud
shots we could find.

Then came the reading. Good as they had been weeks
ago when we cast them, now with their new understanding
of the play and their roles Jim and Nancy were different
people. Actually, they had become Joe and Mary Smith
and once or twice as I listened to the reading I felt embar-
rassed at having intruded on the privacy of these people.
We picked up some more changes, of course; we'd keep
on distilling and refining and improving until the man from
the lab came and took the work print away from us, but it
was ready to go.

I said, "Good-bye, God bless, it's your ball, nine o'clock tomorrow," and they went out.

I doubt if Jim and Nancy and Gary slept too well that night. I know I didn't. And we had plenty of company. In thirty-odd homes from Inglewood to Brentwood, from apartments to bungalows to estates, men and women whose faces would never be seen by an audience were trying to get to sleep against the incessant question which buzzed endlessly against their brains, "Have I missed anything?"

PART THREE

Shooting the Picture

11

You need more than talent to get along in the picture business; you need either an alarm clock or insomnia. It's a business mostly of early rising.

Across the top of Ruby's yellow work order for Tuesday, February 21st, ran the phrase START PRODUCTION. Just below it was a crew call for eight A.M., but the big shadowy stage had started picking up speed an hour before that. Joel Freeman was prowling the set to make sure that everything was ready for the scheduled scenes, plus any and all unexpected curves. Set dressers were pulling the green dust covers off the furnishings and running a vacuum cleaner over the living-room rug. A truck backed in through the big main door, and the $30,000 camera was unloaded and set up on its rubber-tired dolly. The fog drifted in through the door and the air in the stage was raw, but down in the far corner a work light popping up from behind two black flats promised that there would soon be hot coffee.

Bill Wellman strode in about seven-thirty; yellow-covered script rolled up under one arm, black tin dinner-pail hanging from the other. He swapped pleasant insults with some of the crew who had worked with him on previous pictures, lit his pipe, and went over to lay out the first setup with cameraman Bill Mellor. A sound man gave him a "good morning" and kept on tying the microphone to the end of his boom. By now the electricians and grips had checked in, opened their big green stage boxes and begun laying out their equipment. Back by the big door the wardrobe people opened the stars' portable dressing-rooms and racked up "Change No. 1."

For the next few weeks, only the Publicity Department and the front office would recognize the project as *The Next Voice You Hear.* Mostly it would be called "the Wellman company"—sometimes a producer resents being the forgotten man, but during the shooting phase of a picture it's proper that the director carries the flag—and many of the shop and service people would know the picture only by the number 1488 which they would pencil on their job cards.

From its heavy wooden floor to its high flat roof, an active sound stage looks like an impossible conglomeration of clutter. The weird patchwork of floor coverings left over from forgotten kitchens and courtyards is laced with writhing thumb-thick cables, forested with platforms and brackets, studded with a dozen varieties of lights from broads to brutes. Over on one side are grouped the green prop wagon, paint wagon, and the big wooden stage boxes. Above the braced flats which form the sets, big black lamps stare down from the chain-hung scaffolding. These lights have seen everything at one time or another, but at the moment they are staring down at Joe Smith's simple five-room bungalow. From up there, the roofless set looks like a model house in *Life.* In the "practical" set kitchen, prop-man Jimmy Luttrell is squeezing orange juice for the coming scene, and will start coffee as soon as the plumber connects up the gas range.

With Mellor and gaffer Chet Philbrick—the gaffer is

foreman of the electricians, and expert at arranging his equipment to get exactly the lighting effects his cameraman demands—Wellman has been pacing out the physical movements he plans for the opening scene. He decides to angle his master shot from the position of the back door, shooting between the gas range and the refrigerator to "hold" the far wall of the kitchen full width from sink to breakfast nook. Leo Monlon's grips pull out the back-door wild wall and start laying the aluminum track on which the camera dolly will roll in and out as the scene progresses. With the general layout established, gaffer Philbrick sends three of his eleven electricians up into the scaffolding and the rest on the floor equipment. They start roughing in the lighting.

Wellman worries, "If we light this with bright sunlight coming in the window, we'll have to wait for sun tomorrow on location when we shoot the boy going to school." It's a point; the sun is sluggish on February mornings in California. But this breakfast is the first scene of the picture and Bill wants brilliant high-key lighting to set a happy mood in the opening. We'll risk it. Philbrick signals his men to hit the "outdoors" beyond the kitchen windows with the big arcs whose blue-white light simulates daylight.

"Let's have the cast," says Bill. Joel turns toward the portable dressing-rooms and calls for Jim and Nancy. They've come into the stage as unobtrusively as any members of the crew, and now they walk across the floor to the set, Jim in his work clothes and Mary with her pregnancy pad under the red-checkered blouse and blue skirt. Wellman says, "Mary, you'll be sitting at the table cutting off the box-tops. Joe's squeezing the last of the oranges. What's your first line?" And with no more ceremony than that, our epic is on its way. The big 3 ½ -ton doors rumble closed. The time is eight-thirty.

Some directors direct very exhaustively. George Cukor, for example, works at very high pitch and lays out each line and minutest bit of action for his actors in great detail. Others, like Richard Thorpe, seem hardly to direct at all, watching quietly as the actors work up the scene. Wellman is in between. He will dictate exactly what he wants in the way of physical movement and business, but he expects the actors to develop the emotional content of the scene in the way they feel right for their characters. There's no "method," really; each director's way of working reflects his own personality. Bill's volatile, headlong manner charges his actors with his own enthusiasm.

But this first breakfast scene is a challenge to Wellman and his actors alike. As with any scene which holds audience interest, it must be "theater." But that foundational quality of distillation, of projection, must be completely overlaid and absorbed by an atmosphere of seemingly artless, un-rehearsed realism. A very good actor once said, "It's easy to pick up a gun convincingly, very tough to pick up a pencil." Our audiences wouldn't know how to pick up a gun, but they would be experts in how an American family eats breakfast, and this scene would be in trouble at the faintest hint of staginess, self-consciousness, or elocutionary dialogue.

On the first couple of run-throughs Bill was interested only in working out the movement and business, and the over-all tempo; figuring just when Mary will start buttering her bread to have it ready when Joe must take it away from her, what action will pull Joe away from the table to clear the way for the entrance of "the small businessman" from his newspaper route, and so on. Bill wants to inject some freshness in young Johnny's entrance, and a running gag is born. The youngster will stampede in at a headlong pace and slide to a stop. . . . Also, he'll scoot underneath the table and bob up on the far side to dig avidly into his breakfast. By now Mellor knows just about what he'll want in the way of lighting, and Philbrick is working it up. "Kill this junior. Let's get a thousand-watt key light in here. . . . The midget's a little bit hot, add a single net . . . Take the full flood up in the air and let's keep it soft on the girl. . . ."

This scene will run a long three minutes and twenty seconds and is loaded with intricate cross-timings, but the mechanics start rounding into form after two or three runs and Bill begins to work up his reactions and character business. When young Johnny boyishly loads his cereal with sugar, Joe and Mary will notice it and exchange an intimate grin. "You're being too nice, Mary. When Joe pulls the bread away from you, you're burned. Get in some light and shade, so when you do smile at him it will mean something. . . . Look over at that bread as if it were gold." A little later in the scene when Joe picks up his lunch pail, he guesses what is in it and says, "Darling, until you have eaten a cold hamburger sandwich you'll never know how much I love you," but something's a little wrong. Bill tries to figure what. "Mary, you're going to your reaction before the business. If you smile on 'cold hamburger,' what'll you have left when he tickles your ear?" Later: "On the line, 'how much I love you,' " Bill says, "This is the little moment we'll stop for." And, "Don't look up at her, Joe, just keep on shoveling in food—we want business going on all the time, everything piling up on everything, so you don't

seem to be reading dialogue." Mellor is riding the camera
dolly now, his eye to the finder, and signaling for the grips
to push him in and out. Strips of black tape go on the floor
to mark the positions where the camera will stop.

Bill says, "Now I'm beginning to get a little of what I
want—the hurry of breakfast when a man has to get off to
work and the kid's going to school." He goes over to the
camera and hunches forward on the bucket seat, his eye to
the finder as he runs the scene again and shapes it for composition. Finally, it works out to where he knows it will
play the way he wants it to. Joel calls for the second team.
The actors walk off the set and the stand-ins walk in.

Stand-ins, by the way, are not doubles in the sense that
they resemble their principals. There's a general resem-
blance in build and coloring, but that's usually as far as it
goes. A single stand-in may work for many different principals: Jim Whitmore and the late Frank Morgan are to-
tally different in looks, but old-timer Jack Harris used to
represent Morgan and is now standing in for Whitmore.
A "double" is usually hired only for stunt work—Harry
Woolman would double for Jim in the scene where the car
must race backwards out of the driveway—but most doubling is photographed in long-shot and whatever resem-
blance is needed can be handled by wardrobe and makeup.

Stand-ins are not used merely to give the stars a life of
ease; in fact, we supply stand-ins for lesser players. If the
actor were to finish his rehearsal and then have to stand
about for those endless minutes while the lighting is adjusted and the camera moves perfected, he would be tired
and stale when he went into the take and the tiredness
would show.

At nine-twenty-seven Mellor had his lighting up to the

point where he needed a minute or two for final polish with
the principals, and Joel called in the first team. A grip dulled
down a faucet which was bouncing a hot spot of light into
the camera lens, and the standby painter did a similar service on a door jamb which worked like a mirror when
the door swung open. Mellor called, "Okay, Bill," and
walked off. Wellman came back in, camera operator Neal
Beckner climbed into the camera seat, Joel called, "Quiet,
fellows," and the chips went down on the table.

Bill put the scene through one final rehearsal. There were
still some minor rough spots, but the scene was shaking
down into that headlong overlapping tempo he was after,
and he decided to try for a take. Camera and Sound checked
their film loads, the prop man checked his orange juice
and cereal box, and the gaffer signaled his boys to hit their
lights. The big arcs in the background sizzled and fluttered
for a moment as they caught. Neal racked over the camera
and shifted his eyes from the lens to the side-mounted
finder. Matty stepped on the dolly with his hand at the dial
which would alter the focus as the rig moved in. "Let's have
it quiet," called Joel. "This is a take," and the conversa-
tionalists faded slightly. Fred Faust, standing on the boom
which he would crank and twist in and out during the
scene to keep his microphone on top of the dialogue, took
Bill's go-ahead nod and called, "Turn 'em," over his shoulder. From the rear of the crew, mixer Conrad Kahn called
back, "Turning," and thumbed down the fateful red button
on his sound panel.

This button controls a sort of electrical octopus. The
one push starts the sound-film recorder, starts the synchronized camera motor, shuts off the noisy ventilating
fans, cuts off the stage telephone bell, starts the flashing

red light and buzzer outside the stage door, and when the separate strips of film in the camera and recorder have revved up to synchronized operating speed, it fogs sync marks into both strips. In about three seconds it reports success on all these enterprises in the form of a modest buzz.

Connie called, "Speed," and the big stage at last became dead quiet. King Baggot, Jr., poked his scene-chalked slate in front of the lens momentarily. Bill hunched forward and called, "Action." Mary started slitting the cereal box, and *The Next Voice You Hear* was on the road.

On take one Johnny walked through an overlooked hot spot near the stove. Juicers killed a junior and put a silk on one of the broads.* Prop man Jimmy Luttrell adjusted the orange juice and put a new cereal box on the table. On take two Mary bumped into the chair too soon. Jimmy fixed the orange juice and cereal box again. On take three Johnny fluffed his lines about the compass. Phil polished his lighting a little, Neal warned Joe that he went out of camera when he leaned back, and Jimmy took care of his orange juice and cereal box. On each take the crews had smoothed up their handlings a little more, and the actors kept on getting more easy and natural. "Let's try one more," said Bill. "A little more tempo in the eating."

"That's the *one*," said Bill as Mary made her final turn from the window. "Print four and hold two. Any problems?"

Connie the mixer walked in to worry about the noise of plates and spoons over the dialogue, but Bill figured that

---

* *Translation:* Electrical technicians extinguished a miniature spotlight and hung a diffusion fabric over the aperture of an oblong incandescent side-lamp.

it was natural eating sound. "I never heard of people eating off blotters." Script Supervisor Bill Hole had noticed that Joe said *damn* when he spilled some milk, but his lips were off camera and the word was sufficiently clear of other dialogue so that we could paint it out of the track. Still man Eddie Hubbell lugged in his heavy camera to get his publicity stills, the first of several hundred pictures he would snap, and held his ground until he had picked up file-stills of the set and wardrobes; they would be invaluable in the event of re-takes.

Bill lined up the first of his close shots and Mellor began setting up the lighting. Joe and Mary, reverting temporarily to their status as Jim Whitmore and Nancy Davis, walked off set to their portables and Gary Gray trudged across the stage to his canvas-flat school. The time was ten o'clock. For the next three working hours we would shoot parts of the same master scene in thirteen assorted close angles. When these were cut in, probably about thirty seconds of what we had done so far would appear on the screen. Jimmy Luttrell would squeeze oranges in his sleep that night.

The company broke for lunch about twelve-fifteen. The standby car, a long black Chrysler limousine, was waiting at the door, but the sun was out now, the erstwhile empty streets were suddenly colorfully busy, and it was a pleasant walk down through the stages.

Nancy lunched at the commissary with a magazine writer, who didn't know about the ten takes of orange juice and cereal and bread and butter and who formed the mistaken conclusion that Nancy eats like a bird. She does, but it's an eagle.

The commissary is a sunny high-ceilinged restaurant in

which Publicity, Camera, Makeup, Writers and many of
the other departments have long tables of their own,
and smaller tables are scattered about. Lunch prices run
from 50¢ for a salad ("five kinds of lettuce," says Skelton)
to $1.05 for a complete lunch of soup, entree and dessert,
with plenty of extra coffee and candid advice from the
pleasant middle-aged waitresses. Studio policeman Rob
Roy, a diffident ex-wrestler who unobtrusively guards the
door, knows practically every one of the 3,500 employees by name and what time they usually come down to
lunch.

12

Back at Stage 18 Bill Wellman has robbed the prop wagon of some of the breakfast eggs and bacon and is calmly scrambling a lunch on the practical gas range in the kitchen set for himself and cameraman Mellor. Outside, propped against the walls in the sun, lounges the lunch-pail contingent. Jim Whitmore is a sandwich-thermos-apple guy, but mostly these men are members of the mechanical crews attached to the shooting company: grips, electricians and greensmen.

In looks they're a typical slice of American craftsmen, except that they seem easier in manner and somehow more "individual." Standard dress seems to be slacks or work pants, with an open-neck sport shirt or T-shirt. The ages run mostly between thirty-five and the late fifties, with an accent on the elder bracket, and most of them have worked at this one studio ten years or more, including old-timers who stood a few yards from this very spot a quarter century ago during the merger ceremonies and wondered whether the new company would make the grade. This is a business where the years of personal experience have a cash value: many an on-set emergency is averted by an older man who can remember "that John Gilbert deal in the schooner cabin—seems to me we bounced the light around the corner off a mirror."

These men draw hourly pay rates higher than for similar work outside, on the union philosophy that movie employ-

ment is "day call" work and hence sporadic. True, the cas-
uals who come into the studio only on temporary calls do
badly for annual income, but these regulars whom the
studio tries to keep busy as its "hard core" of steady employees mostly take in around $100 a week for a minimum
of forty weeks per year (overtime may boost this to
$150 and more when companies are shooting). The weekly
$208.25 of the key grips and gaffers puts them in the
$10,000 executive class. Whether we can maintain these
standards when we encounter the full force of television
competition and divorcement of our theatres, nobody can
say.

But I can say that these men contribute a kind of work
which has vanished from too many American industries—
cheerful, willing, alert work by men who seem to feel themselves personally responsible for the entire project, who
look around for things that need to be done and "jump to
it" without orders, men who are crack at their jobs and
casually proud of it. This spirit is not confined to the major
studios. I have seen the same jump and zest in quickie companies on Poverty Row. The wellspring of this old-fashioned spirit might well be looked into by industries which
are suffering from low worker productivity.

Many of the several hundred men in Frank Barnes' Grip
Department do their work behind the scenes. They do the
sewing and placing of all canvas, from the huge painted
backings which reproduce exteriors inside the stages, to
"tarping in" acres of outdoor sets when a director wants
to shoot night scenes in the straight-rate daylight hours.
Grips also hang those miles of open scaffolding for lighting
platforms around the perimeter of all sets.

But the glamour boys of the department are the "company grips" like Leo Monlon's gang on *Next Voice*. They operate the sets. Their badge is the wide leather belt slung low over the hips, from which depend gloves, hammer and rolls of tape and wire; over a sturdy apron whose pockets contain pliers, cutters, screw-drivers, knives, crescent wrenches, steel tape, chalk, assorted nails, cigarettes and Chiclets.

Grips are the company handymen. Jurisdiction over a physical set passes from the construction unions to the grips as soon as the camera grinds its first frame, and from then on they move the walls and take care of set alterations. Taking orders from the cameraman, they place all shade, diffusion and reflectors; they lay the camera track for moving shots, and manage all propulsion of the camera. This latter function occasionally enlists a boatman or helicopter pilot, but most of the men came into the department from the labor gang, most of them with past experience "on the outside" in carpentry, plumbing, painting, and other trades.

Company electricians are artists with strong backs. It's the job of silver-haired, stocky Chet Philbrick to deliver whatever lighting effects his cameraman instructs, and to do it fast, because lighting the sets takes up more of that precious production time than any other company operation.

Lighting a movie is a science which goes far beyond merely "fixing it so you can see the people." It even carries an important share of the actual story-telling, by silently keying the mood of a scene, implying the time of day and state of the weather, subtly accenting objects the audience should notice, restoring youth to aging stars and, particularly, creating the illusion of a third dimension in what otherwise would be a two-dimensional medium.

If you hold your finger directly under a light, you'll notice it seems flat: now move your finger beside the light, and see how the side shadow brings out its roundness. The motion-picture screen is an absolutely flat surface, and the picture itself gains the illusion of depth and roundness and contour because of the skillful and artistic placing of light and shadow. Look at the back walls in the next movie you see, and notice the deliberate designs of shadows thereon. Those background shadows separate the background from the foreground, they seem to push out foreground objects to compel the illusion of depth. You can notice the lack of this separation lighting in most of today's live-show television. Home-movie cameramen take notice.

Hobbyists might also profit from another studio practice. Studio crews light for "positions": that is, they place equipment to illuminate each of the actors in a scene for each position in which he stays put for any length of time. In practice, the experienced director plans the scene to keep the number of these positions within reason. But each position must be lit so that it looks like a portrait, and a scene with four actors, each with three moves, really amounts to lighting twelve painstaking portrait sittings. And the real object of all this care is to make sure that the lighting and photography will not be noticed, that all the audience's attention will go to the actors.

The lighting in a scene begins with the "key light," the apparent source of whatever light illuminates the scene. It may be the sun or moon through a window, a light fixture on the wall or ceiling or table, a cigarette lighter in the hand, or whatever, but everything is built from there to give the impression that all the enormous amount of light which must flood the scene for good photography—at the rate of twenty-four exposures per second—comes from that key source. The juicers have a language all their own, and some of it makes wonderful hearing: "Feed that broad through the door. Tip it up so it doesn't hit the jamb, full flood. . . . Try a single silk, bring the top door down a little and gobo the baby spot. . . . Take all the junk off that junior in the hall; gimme a little shaft of light out through the door. . . . I want to just miss the seat of this chair. . . . Some light is leaking over the door. . . . Swing the one with the snoot for a little backlight on Mary—it's too hot— we'll have to net her down, a drip net if we can get away with it. . . . We can use a baby on a stick over here. . . . Okay, that's it, save 'em." Philbrick can grow lyric as he describes the lighting of a scene involving blowy fog at night under a lonely street lamp in the snow.

His hour of trial, however, comes when his men must hit or kill twenty huge arcs in absolute synchronism as an actor blows out a candle or something. Every juicer in town saw Warner Brothers' *June Bride,* but not many of them joined in the roars of laughter when Robert Montgomery trotted about a room snapping out lamp after lamp and Bette Davis followed after him switching them on again.

Some of the electricians' work is brutally hard, particularly that phase of the rigging crews known as "hauling iron." This is the job which comes after the grips have hung the scaffolding, of sweating half-ton arc lights and festoons of heavy cables up above the set with block and falls. The crew call for a rigging job often coincides with an epidemic of vague illness which decimates the available electricians, an epidemic which miraculously clears up when the set is "lined" and ready for operation. Chet's assistant, Howard Roberts, whose job carries the odd title of Best Boy, is expert at diagnosing such ailments. Over the years Chet and Howard have become adept at handling anything, from fire in the cables to rigging a three-hundred-pound drunk down a vertical ladder from a sixty-foot high catwalk. Incidentally, drunkenness and derelictions of duty are dealt with within the union itself, with discipline more severe than any employer would dare enforce. Of course, discipline does have its limits. After all, since heated air is always going to rise toward the roof, the cliffhangers tending the high arcs are occasionally going to fall asleep and let their funny papers sail down into the middle of tense emotional scenes. One gaffer kept this situation under control for some years with a sling-shot, but this method is not now considered enlightened management practice.

Anything that grows from earth is the concern of Walter Fabel's "Greens" department. From the thousands of plant varieties on his twenty acres of glass, slat and open ground nurseries, Walter can supply in a matter of minutes anything from an Egyptian date palm to a vine orchid or an acre of growing wheat.

Like the studio lumberyard which keeps its new stock in the open and padlocks beaten-up wood that anyone else would burn, Fabel's most carefully guarded plants are such weedy items as the marsh grass and dandelions toward which art directors' fancies always seem to turn in January. Every studio has a standing order for several truck loads each morning of fresh-cut leafy shrubs and tree branches, some of them for nailing to plaster boughs in the fabricating of trees, but more to be fastened on brackets in front of stage lights to cast the vague leafy shadows which unobtrusively mark depth on the background.

Most of the greensmen's work on sets is finished before shooting starts, and the men are wonderful on the tiny details which add up to reality. "A little weed here, a tuft of grass growing up between the planks of the board walks, the stuff a little greener around the bottom of a watering trough where the ground would get damp," says Fabel, "audiences don't consciously notice those things, but they make a lot of difference." The potato hills of the vegetable gardens in *King Solomon's Mines* are twice the normal height so that they will cast the shadows by which they will make their presence known.

It's the duty of prop man Jimmy Luttrell, last seen squeezing orange juice, to think of, procure, keep ready, and guard from theft the multitude of portable items which appear in a film. "All the departments have their grief and responsibility," says Jimmy, "but we got all this junk, too."

Jimmy's pre-production breakdown of hand props listed not only what the script came right out and called for, but whatever else a director like Billy Wellman might think of when he read it. A scene calls for a basket but, Jimmy thinks, "Bill might decide to use a satchel." In addition to the oranges and cereal boxes, Jimmy's breakdown listed such items as a newsboy's bag, potato peelings, dry ice (for silent steam in tea kettle), mud (to track into house), hymn books, and lunch boxes. Jimmy takes a craftsman's pride at never being caught short of any prop, no matter how exotic, whether the script lists it or not. The two large green-painted chests on set which hold his personal packrat's paradise contain four thousand different items ranging from alarm clocks to zwieback. If Jimmy lacks an item, he will adapt something else to the purpose: a peppermint Lifesaver once made a convincing bunion plaster, and a cake of Parowax cut up into camera-proof "ice cubes."

Jimmy is expected to set all clocks which appear in scenes, to tuck in any heroines who appear in bedroom scenes, and to "age" the newness out of practically every prop that appears in the picture. For the aircraft factory scene in *Next Voice* Jimmy had to buy fifty lunch boxes. While he was brooding about how to go about aging all these shiny new creations, one of the fellows displayed the battered specimen he had been carrying to work the last dozen years and kidded, "Wanna swap even?" That he did. The word zoomed around the back lot, and in two hours Jimmy had the town's best collection of veteran lunch boxes. Including Wellman's.

Jimmy's nemesis is the screen writer who blithely types such phrases as, "Father begins to carve the turkey." To a prop man, this means that he must have on set at nine A.M. at least a half-dozen whole fresh-roasted turkeys (with provision to keep same steaming) so that Father can sink his knife into virgin skin in each of the possibly numerous takes. Once when a screen writer treated his characters to a fish dinner and the scene ran into unexpected difficulties, Jimmy ran out of complete fish and had to sew the severed portions back together for the final take. Which is why you don't see many eating scenes in low-budget pictures, unless, of course, it is something simple like orange juice and cold cereal.

The lunch break ended at one-fifteen and most everybody was back on deck a few minutes before that.

13

It was about half-past three when the final pickup on the second kitchen scene went into the can. Joel called, "We're in the wrong set, boys," and the company moved around to INT. JOHNNY'S BEDROOM. In the mimeographed script, the scene read like this:

MARY, JOHNNY—*Interior Johnny's room*, night   22

At a small desk-table, Johnny in pajamas and robe struggles with his homework. We hear o.s. sound of radio, faintly.
JOHNNY (*mumbling*)
Bring down the nine—another nine!
He chews his pencil. The offstage sound of the radio stops abruptly. Mary becomes aware of the silence, puzzles about it briefly, goes back to the homework. The door opens. Joe stands in the doorway. He seems mildly disturbed, rubs the back of his neck with his palm.
MARY
What is it, Joe?
Joe just shakes his head.
MARY
Finish the dishes?
JOE
Huh? Oh, sure—yeah . . .
MARY
You're not listening to the radio—what's wrong?
JOE
Kind of a funny thing—on the radio—they announced it was exactly eight-thirty . . .
JOHNNY
Garry Gavery—the Golden-Voiced Goon . . .

MARY

Quiet, Johnny.

JOE

Yeah. They announced it. Then there was kind of an odd empty sound. Then a voice said, "This is God. I will be with you for the next few days."

Joe finishes with a wonder in his voice.

MARY

What?

JOE (*puzzled*) A voice said, "This is God. I will be with you for the next few days."

MARY (*a moment*) Then what happened?

JOE

Nothing happened—the program came back on. . . .

MARY

Maybe it was just the introduction . . .

JOE

No—because when the program did come on again, Garry Gavery was smack in the middle of his first song.

Mary thinks hard for a moment, comes up with an answer.

MARY

It must be one of those Mystery Voice shows—you have to guess whose voice . . .

JOE

But they never do that unless they tell you all about the prizes. . . .

MARY

Or maybe one of those Orson Welles things . . .

JOHNNY

I got it! It was little Eddie Boyle! He's always trying to be a radio ham—maybe he cut in . . .

JOE

Well, if that isn't the silliest . . . Would Eddie Boyle's voice sound like God?

JOHNNY

I don't know. I never heard God.

MARY (*to Johnny*)
That's not very nice, Johnny. Go to bed.
JOE
Yeah . . .
  (*He turns, exits to living room*)
  Mary looks after Joe a moment, then turns to Johnny.
MARY
Go ahead, Johnny. Get undressed.
  She turns, follows Joe out and closes the door.
                                              DISSOLVE TO:

Good acting is not spontaneous, though it must always
seem to be. The lines of dialogue in the script are only the
surface shell of a scene, and a competent actor immediately
digs under them to find his "attitude" and his objective.
Joe's attitude would be puzzled. Also he'd be ninety-nine
percent skeptical about the voice being God's—but that
one percent trace would be enough to plant the fear which
must start to grow tomorrow. Young Johnny is skeptical
and "So what?" Mary, too, is puzzled. But there is a little
more stirring of fear deep within her—which she smothers
under her instinctive woman's reaction, "Keep the home
going." The over-all mood of the scene would be subdued,
and the two adults would underplay.

On the first run-through, Wellman and the actors began
converting these intangibles into physical business, for the
actor's horror is a scene which requires him just to stand
there, in the professional phrase, "with egg on his face."
This need of physical business accounts for a good deal of
the cigarette lighting and drink lifting in movies, these being the first devices the uninventive director seems to think
of when his actors are standing like shop-window manne-
quins as they bat lines back and forth. The basic business

was built into this scene right at the beginning, with
Johnny bending over his homework at the desk, Mary
mending as she watches, and the two of them pricking up
their ears when the radio fades down and looking toward
the door when Joe enters. Later, at Joe's "this is God" line,
Johnny would look up and Mary lay down her mending,
and the emotional tension would be so tight from there on
that nothing more would be needed.

If good acting must seem spontaneous, good direction
must seem like no direction at all. Bill's whole effort is to
wipe away all trace of his own participation so that the
eventual scene looks as though a roving camera had poked
in and caught the people unaware. A typical instruction
from him is, "You're anticipating Mary's interruption—
the audience will think you're turning because the director
told you to."

But there is no question as to who is in charge on a Wellman set. Volatile, explosive, outspoken, thin and hard as
a coil of wire, his mobile left eyebrow often cocked in
amusement or indignation, he gives the impression that he
knows exactly what he wants and is most certainly going
to get it. This is wonderful for the cast and crew. It's an
awful feeling on a set where the people are uncertain, but
there's none of it around a Wellman company; everybody
rocks along at full gait in the cheerful confidence that papa
knows best. Sometimes I think Bill is the most completely
natural and uninhibited human being in the universe; at
others I wonder if he isn't really the most canny of poseurs,
with every explosion and change in temperature expertly
calculated. One thing I am sure of, nothing he does is for
personal vanity, not ever; it's all for the picture. He cajoles
and bullies and flatters and curses and babies and drives his

cast like a master psychologist, and they love him and resent him and give him twice what they've got. But I do
know of one moment when Bill is absolutely himself, without calculation, and that's when he hunches over the camera operator as a scene is going into the can: mouth open,
tongue licking, body twisting and eyes tortured, he's pulling what he wants out of his people by sheer, mystic power
of will.

Bill okayed the master shot on the third take, and the
crew shifted into second gear for that tedious phase of the
movie-maker's job, getting the "pickups." Though an audience should never realize it, a scene like this one in Johnny's bedroom, not particularly lengthy, will reach the
screen as a composite of clips shot from several varying
distances and angles. The purpose isn't merely to give variety; most of the pickups are close shots of one or two people which the cutter inserts into the longer-distance master
to satisfy the audience's curiosity as to characters' reactions
and emotions, and to put over important plot points.

The pickup shots use a good deal of time, often more
time than is needed to shoot the master, and hence they
account for a good deal of the cost of a picture. The next
time you see a B picture on the lower half of a double bill,
it might be interesting to note the paucity of close shots,
the small number of bit scenes and flashes, "establishment
shots" of exteriors, reverse angles, and "geography" long
shots. Note also the bits of awkwardness and unnatural
action which one or two more takes might have smoothed
out. The real reason why poor quality is undesirable is that
it calls attention to itself, whereas good quality lets the audience enjoy the play and the players to the full without
mechanical distraction.

Bill wanted five pickups on this scene to supplement 22A, the full shot master which was already in the can. 22B was a medium close shot of Joe as he entered the bedroom door, to catch his puzzled uncertainty. 22C was a face closeup of Joe. In 22D, the side wall came out and the camera favored Mary, shooting across young Johnny at the desk, to catch her growing worry. 22E was the same except that it was a closeup of Mary alone, with Joe and Johnny delivering their lines from outside the camera field. 22F came in close on young Johnny at his desk to pick up his reaction to Joe's first report of the Voice saying *this is God*, and to emphasize his climax line of the scene, "I don't know. I never heard God." The cutter would not use all the footage in these; in fact, each shot duplicated basic action in another, but he would have an ample selection. And the scene would be protected in case we changed our minds or preview audiences later on disagreed with our judgment as to what was important.

Since the whole bedroom had already been master-lighted for all the positions, these pickups went rapidly. Chet killed the big overhead lights except those which lit the particular position being picked up, and floor lights were quickly brought in and adjusted. The stand-ins did their stints, Matty held his tape measure impersonally in the stars' faces as Chet cuddled his light-meter in their ears, and one by one the shots were ready to work up.

Every pickup shot involves some questions about "matching." Obviously, when the final film makes an instantaneous cut from a long shot to the same actor in closeup, the actor must be doing exactly the same thing in both shots even though they may have been photographed several hours apart. It is the actor's obligation, and one that calls for extraordinary skill, to recreate his posture, facial expression, pace, intonation, and inner emotion exactly. But many questions also arise as to items of fact, and these go to the Script Supervisor.

The script supervisor on *Next Voice* was a slight, dark-haired young man with a stop-watch dangling from a cord around his neck and a leather-bound script hooked in the crook of his elbow. His name is Bill Hole, and he is in charge of not getting letters—that is, he is responsible for preventing noticeable boners such as the milk bottle which fills and empties by magic from cut to cut, the dress which changes its pattern, the clock which gains an hour between reverse angles of the same scene, the glance to the left which sees something to the right, the feet which walk out of a doorway in slippers and enter the next room in shoes —all those pitfalls which threaten when action is shot out of straight continuity.

Hole blocks off these unhappy occurrences by a process of uncannily detailed observation of everything that happens on every take, penciling the salient points thereof on his script for later reference so that he can pass along the reminder, "You had your hand in your pocket before you reached for the door," or, "You pointed your index finger toward Johnny's paper when he said *Another nine*," or, "Johnny's hair was hanging down over his forehead in the long shot." He also serves as a dialogue director, to the extent of prompting the actors in rehearsing, and he checks all dialogue in the takes. As a sort of camera historian he keeps a record of the lens through which each take was photographed, a diagram of where the sidelines fell on the set in each shot, plus the footages exposed. And his minute-by-minute log of the day's progress includes some fascinating indications of where the time and money go.

He makes $125 a week, works six long days a week when "in production," usually spends some evening time keeping his complex records up to date, and goes to sleep with the invariable question, "Did I miss anything?" Two seconds of inattention at the wrong time can cost the worth of a yacht in retakes. But since it's his job to watch Bill Wellman's every move and read his reasoning, to diagram the physical movement in each scene and the camera handling thereof, Bill Hole is in an ideal spot to learn the art of directing, and he may some time get his chance through the intermediate steps of second assistant director ($140), assistant ($262), and unit manager ($300).

While the earlier pickup shots were being ground out, Ruby Rosenberg had come up to the stage from the Production Office and was huddling around the telephone pulpit and the high stage desk with the two assistant directors. The day was far enough along now so that they could decide what scenes could be set up for tomorrow. They went over the schedule and script to list what people and facilities would be required. Then Ruby took the information back to his cubbyhole and typed up the yellow sheets of tomorrow's work order which, listing the scenes to be shot and the sets to be used, would notify each department what time to report, with what equipment, and what it must be prepared to do.

Ex studio schoolteacher Fletcher Clark, the second assistant, used the same information to get out The Three-o'clock-Report—the mimeographed white sheets which would list the actors, stand-ins and doubles, type and num-

ber of extras to be called for tomorrow, together with the
wardrobe changes they should wear and the numbers of
the scenes they should study. A copy of it would go by
teletype to Central Casting to line up the extras. Ruby had
been in a meeting at eleven A.M. with the unit managers
and art directors of all the other shooting companies, so
he knew that his plans would not trip over anybody
else's. These particular orders were mostly routine contin-
uations of today's work, except for changes of wardrobe,
and instructions to Electrical to prepare a "Scissors" for
the lightning effect.

Wellman called "Print that one" on the final pickup a
few minutes before six. The three actors went to their portables, thankful that they didn't have to take off makeup and
unglue hair pieces; electricians and grips began gathering
up their scattered equipment and organizing it for the next
day, Bob Streeter and Florance Hackett picked up the
wardrobe changes and returned them to the costume lines
for overnight freshening, Jimmy Luttrell gave away his
leftover oranges and locked up his working props in the
stage box, Camera and Sound wrapped up their equipment
and checked back to their headquarters, the assistant directors began telephoning tomorrow's calls to the actors listed
on the "three-o'clock," and Wellman took five minutes to
lay out the morning's first setup with Mellor before he
picked up his lunch pail and headed down the dark studio
street for home.

The log credited the day's work with four scenes, shot
in twenty-one camera setups. Bill had crossed off eight
pages of his script; Mellor had exposed 4,690 feet of film,
of which 500 feet would appear on the screen for a running
time of five and one-half minutes. This would be consid-

ered fast work on anybody's lot, but it was particularly
fast for what we hoped would be a quality picture. Bill was
shaking down the cast and crew into a tight, hot unit. It
began to look as though we might make the twenty-two
day shooting schedule.

The night crews of two or three men each came up from
Grips and Greens to put back the wandering wild walls as
they were positioned on the set blueprint, and freshen the
shrubbery around the front "exterior" of the house. A
painter squinted around the walls to touch up any spot a
lamp might have scraped or a boom dented. Along about
nine they packed up, shut off the high stage lights, and trundled their carts of materials and tools back to where they
came from.

The big door yawned open and the busy stage slept, vast
and shadowy and cavernous. The magic was wrapped up
for the night.

14

By Friday, when the company moved into the locker-room set, it had shaken down into a comfortable unit, knit together into a "we" morale by mutual liking and an accumulation of private jokes. For Jeff Corey and big Tom d'Andrea, Joe's factory pals, today was the first work day. But like most Hollywood supporting and character players, they settled into place and became part of the company in a matter of minutes.

There is a playwrighting axiom to the effect that any line should do one of three things: advance the plot, develop character, or get a laugh—"laugh" in the sense of any desired audience emotion. In movies, where we must present the equivalent of a novel or a play in around ninety minutes, we must try to make each line and bit do all three jobs at once. And so, since the dialogue would take care of advancing the plot, Wellman kept digging for chances to flesh out the characters and build the laughs.

The script had given the irascible foreman, Mr. Brannan, a running line which he used frequently when his men were dallying in the locker room: "An honest day's work for an honest dollar." On the first appearance of the line, Wellman kept the camera on Brannan, to get the line established. But the next time the line came in he wanted it to perform that triple duty, and he cast about for some hearer's reaction to which he could cut. Sardonic Tom d'Andrea would be a good bet. What would be Tom's reaction to the line? He'd

be fed up, hating this slavedriver and thinking, "Every day
it's the same old stuff." Fine. But by what bit of physical
business would Tom make his unspoken thoughts visible?

In the answer is the clue to how the great running gags
and bits of business come into being. Bill's simple but very
funny and characterful answer was to have Tom's mouth
do a different pantomime imitation of the words whenever
Brannan spoke the phrase. It's always a chuckle on the
screen, and the time Brannan almost catches him it's a sure
roar.

Bill would invariably phone me, as the producer, after
he had shot one of these inventions and say, "I cooked up
something today, I don't know if it's going to work." Almost always I'd like what he'd done; his inventiveness, gov-
erned by his instinctive taste and discrimination, was the
primary quality for which I'd wanted him on the picture.
But in this business, when a man's stuff is perfect it's often
a sign that he's playing everything too safe, not taking
enough swings at the chancy ones. So if I disagreed with
something, all I had to do was begin, "Well, Billy, I'm not
so sure . . ." and he would instinctively know just what
bit had bothered me, because, although he might have re-
sisted his subconscious feeling, it had bothered him, too.

Another effective running gag got in by accident. "You
three men are standing around too long," Bill worried toward the finish of a scene. So he had Joe and Jeff try picking up their tool trays and walking out of the locker room
while Tom was still speaking his curtain line.

It solved the spot problem, but Wellman's directorial eye
kept going and he saw what he could build out of it. "Hey,
that can be good, Tom," he said. "You're always walking
out behind the others saying something funny and they're

Nancy Davis awaits her fate at her audition reading From left Director
Bill Wellman, Producer Dore Schary and co-star James Whitmore

Pre-production cast rehearsal. Director Wellman indicates action for his
stars on the set diagram

The first scene on the schedule Joe young Johnny and Mary Smith at breakfast

A painted scenic backing reproduces the location exterior as seen from Joe Smith's front door

Assistant cameraman checks focus for a close shot.

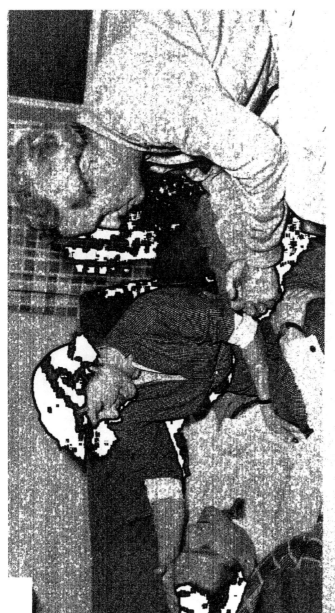

Director Wellman gets in close to work out the shading of an intimate emotional scene

The locker-room cast work out the scene while the set is being lighted.

Working out the action on a location exercise

A typical stage crew at work

Grips move a section of "wild wall" out of camera field

Associate Art Director Eddie Imazu checks the model of the "Fat Branin Back Yard" set

Electricians handle the lights, grips supply the shade. Head Grip Leo Moulon at far left, Gaffer Chet Philbrick in center

Set Decorator Ralph Hurst seems to be in the wrong Prop Room for
The Next Voice

An actor's-eye view of the stage sound crew Boom Man Fred Faust and
Mixer Conrad Kahn.

'I cooked up something today See what you think of it' Dore Schary,
Eddie Imazu and Bill Wellman

Lunch on location

The Smith family: Joe, Mary, and young Johnny.

paying no attention to you." Typical of Wellman's touches, there was nothing gaggy about it; it probably happens every day in every factory in the country.

As a matter of fact, the locker-room set and factory routine was not as out of place on a movie lot as you might think. Like a self-contained city, the studio has its own industrial section, appropriately located down by the railroad track in a conglomerate array of Topsyish structures collectively known as the back lot. Most of the shops are small, reminiscent of the cottage crafts of medieval times, but the uncannily skilled artisans who work in them turn out a greater variety of stranger items in smaller quantities and in faster time than any other group on earth. Quite literally, they will make anything or a photogenic facsimile thereof.

At first glance, everything seems quite normal. The plumbing shop is a plumbing shop. The hardware shop contains a lot of everyday hardware to offset the great castle drawbridge hinges now on the bench. The brightly lit carpenter shop is spotted with standard woodworking machines, smells of sawdust and varnish, and could be making furniture or prefab housing. But then your eyes drift to a group of gentlemen methodically sawing up brand-new automobile bodies like slices of bread. Suddenly you notice that most of the nails have two heads, one above the other. But just as someone explains it's only because they pull out with less damage when sets are struck, somebody else mentions that the man was in about renting the snake, and you are back again in a world where it seems logical when people complain, "It's driving me normal." This is only the beginning.

In a color-slopped upstairs sign shop, Chris Smith and

his artists will letter free-hand anything from the signboard for a 1492 Spanish inn sign to *Happy 4th of July* on thirty-six young ladies' stomachs.

Jack Pollyea's fabulously cluttered paper props storeroom smells like a second-hand book store and supplies the company prop men with menus and mortgages, labels and licenses, posters and programs, stamps and scorecards and everything else on paper, plus undertakers'-convention badges on silk and Coolidge buttons on celluloid. Jack's packrat proclivities—he embarrasses his wife whenever they go out in public by stealing anything with printing on it—have enriched all of his twenty filing categories except one, the Bond-and-Currency drawer.

Bob Tittle's paint department keeps $50,000 worth of paint on hand, uses five times that much annually, and spends upwards of $2,000 a day for labor alone. No cottage craft this, with gang pushers spotting their brush crews all over the studios, painting whole buildings and sets big and small. But in no other industry would a painter make zebras out of donkeys in the morning, and paddle a raft around a huge indoor tank in the afternoon spilling just enough bottled household bluing to tint the water the proper Technicolor blue for Esther Williams. If he uses more than one quart of bluing to the 800,000 gallons of water, the girls in the swimming ballet will emerge with blue hair. He found this out.

A man can achieve studio fame more quickly in the paint department than anywhere else. There is a legendary character named Spraygun Miller: when he sprays a wall he sprays everything on it, even a sweater. Cheerful Frank Wesselhoff, the standby painter on *Next Voice*, was recently spraying shrubbery to a Technicolor green and forgot to shut off the sprayer as he turned away, with the result that he painted a foot-wide stripe across the director, cameraman and crew. Later on in *Next Voice* Wellman asked Frank to spray the hands of a cop black to look like gloves, but Frank demurred, "I don't paint people on purpose. I only paint people by accident." And it was a painter from another studio entirely who went down to Balboa in advance of his company and spent two days doing a memorable aging job on the wrong yacht.

But despite all the ribbing, it was Frank, the brim of his battered canvas hat pushed up in front and brushes sticking out of every pocket of his splattered white pants, whose skill and watercolors aged down the shoes of the too-trim workers on the Douglas location, who quickly "made" a piece of patterned wallpaper that couldn't be told from the torn original, and who knew how to "bring down" the sun-reflecting rear of a location house with alcohol and dry colors which would dry instantly without shine. In the paint shop itself, other skillful men brush the convincing color surface on such unorthodox items as breakaway pies and polo mallets of foam rubber, twelve full-size plastic harps, and a full-size plaster dinosaur.

Many of these breakaways, gags, and imitations come from Lee Crawford's rubber room. His boys made the gigantic ears and tusks which transformed an Indian elephant into his African cousin for *King Solomon's Mines*, and the rubber steering wheels to protect race-driver Gable in *To Please a Lady*. In this same shop, George Lofgren has developed a way to transfer any real animal fur surface from its original stiff hide to stretchable rubber film, very useful for the mechanical animals we must use in process-screen closeups. George goes down to Mexico shortly to get the hide of a fighting bull which he will mechanize for some of the close shots in *Quo Vadis*.

There are two special achievements down on this part of the lot at the moment. One is a completely new kind of foam rubber, which can be colored right in the mix, cast in molds to any shape, and will float. They're using it for the beautiful array of Technicolor sea plants through whose waving fronds Miss Williams and her girls will swim in a *Pagan Love Song* ballet.*

The other item is a way of using a plastic called laminac with glass fiber to make feather-light and practical reproductions of all sorts of things, from ornamental castle doors and ship masts to carved mantels and flexible tree bark. We expect this to replace the plaster work which has been invaluable to us for so many years. The plastic will take color in the mix so that a dent doesn't require repainting, and is waterproof for exterior use. Take one of those tall columns which grace the entrance to a Roman temple or a Southern mansion. In marble it would weigh many tons. Plaster brings the weight down to the couple of tons which we can handle, but the new plastic column weighs fifty pounds and can be put in place by one man. Like so much of the inventiveness here on the back lot, it lets us bring you authentic sights which you would never otherwise see.

Paradoxically, the plaster-shop crew is busier than ever. Their work is called "Staff" for some long-forgotten reason, and propped against the walls to dry in the sun outside their white-powdered building are all sorts of objects you would never expect to see made of plaster. Staff's bread-

* Miss Williams pokes a shivery toe in the water before she goes in all over, just like anybody else. Her durable underwater coiffure is sprayed with Plastic Wipe-On, more usually applied to linoleum.

and-butter work, cast up ahead of time and stacked in the warehouse, are the big square panels of all manner of brickwork and stonework, field boulders, roof slates, skyscraper limestone, and carved "wooden" paneling. When the painters finish off the surfaces, these panels will be completely convincing even to the close up naked eye, though their joints are cut deeper than true to cast those essential shadows for the camera. Ray Davies and his men are currently rushing out 300 classic miniature buildings and statues for Nero's spectacular burning of Rome in *Quo Vadis*. Rome may not have been built in a day originally, but Staff will rebuild it, with carefully researched authenticity, in about three weeks.

Adjoining the Staff shop, the high glassy space which looks amazingly like a sculptor's studio is a sculptor's studio. In it, Henry Greutert and his men model the hundreds of needed objects which cannot be conveniently cast from an original. Into this classification fall many objects the private sculptors never even heard of. The contours for a mechanical horse, for instance, those hinges for the castle drawbridge, the lacy ironwork of a New Orleans balcony, wooden Indians, and the backbone of a half-eaten fish.

In all these back-lot shops the fantastic versatility has to be coupled with a speed which craftsmen in any other industry would consider ridiculous; it keeps reminding me of a wonderful bit of understatement in a production manual which read: "Since in the motion-picture business, lack of time is mostly the case." If you remember the huge statue of the buffalo at the World's Fair in *Meet Me in St. Louis*, you'll be interested to know that Henry modeled the twelve-inch original, set up the twenty-foot-high skeleton-like armature, slapped on nobody knows how many tons of clay, and had the gigantic piece ready for the truck in ten days from the date of the Art Director's requisition.

Partitioned off in a corner of Stage 10 is the leather shop. Burly Lee Lampkin, craggy and aproned like Longfellow's village blacksmith, was once a harness-maker for Buffalo Bill Cody. He felt as though he were repeating himself this year when he tooled the leather and chased the silver mountings for the boots and saddles and belts and scabbards in *Annie Get Your Gun*. Hanging on the musty shop walls are all manner of weird contraptions. There is the concealed piano wire harness which protected *Kim* when he slipped from the mountain cliff, the "hunchback" which Jim Whitmore wore in *Asphalt Jungle*, and the dress shoes weighted with eighteen pounds of lead in each sole which frustrated Spencer Tracy in the riotous dream sequence of *Father of the Bride*.

Lampkin's tools cost over $7,000 and include forty-one different kinds of scissors. These tools wear rapidly, and once every few weeks Lee bundles them up, throws in all his scrap ends of leather and patterns, and pays the express on them to a destination in Nebraska which he happened across while doing another picture some years ago—*Boys' Town*. Lee makes no fuss about it. I found it out by accident. Just as I found out about budgeteer Joe Finn's hobby of raising money to combat juvenile delinquency by lighting school playgrounds at night. And about Charlie Cochrane, chief of tabulating, whose record of boys' work includes training the first blind boy to become an Eagle Scout. And about Saul Scher of Sound Effects, who badgers every star and location manager in town to get the foreign envelopes from their fan mail for his "Stamps

for the Wounded" collectors in the veterans' hospitals. And
a lot more.

The white-haired gunsmith who literally holds the fort
upstairs over the construction office is Lee Constable, and
the 1,500 weapons in his gun room trace the progress of
warfare from tomorrow's rocket pistol back to French
arquebuses and Indian blowguns. Lee is whittling out the
stock for a flintlock derringer at the moment, and complaining that things have been quiet around the place since
Annie went away.

Lee and powder-man Andy Parks had a field day devis-
ing and operating the "gags"—meaning mechanical gadgets
or methods, not necessarily funny—to help 30,000,000
theatregoers accept the illusion that Betty Hutton was the
greatest markswoman of all time. Since film audiences always suspect trickery, often wrongly, you can't nowadays
fire the gun in a closeup and cut away to a different shot
of the target being shattered; gun and target must appear
simultaneously in the same picture. So Miss Hutton's deadly
accuracy was dubbed in by a professional marksman standing just off the sidelines with a compressed air gun, or by
an electrical connection between Betty's trigger and an explosive squib implanted in the target, or other means.

There was typical Yankee ingenuity in the scene of Betty
shooting up the Technicolor glass balls which the Indians
threw in the air. The balls, filled with photographers' flash
powder and colored pigment, were built on the principle
of wartime hand grenades, and the Indians pulled out the
pins but held down the levers until time to throw the balls
in the air, where they would explode a couple of seconds

after being tossed upwards. One Indian did not remember about holding down the lever and will never trust a white man again.

In an annex off the rubber room works slight, hard-bitten, razor-minded Max Geuppinger. Holder of a university doctorate in optics, astronomer, chemist, physicist, electronic expert (for relaxation, he makes Geiger counters), Jack of many trades and master of all, Max is referred to, purely for a simplified handle, as the Glassblower. Did you happen to see the man-size transparent malted milk mixer in which *Yellow Cab Man* Skelton got trapped? Max made it. No one has ever really seen himself until he has stood in front of one of Max's "surface mirrors," which carry the silvering on the front face of the glass. And no wintry exterior set is complete without a few blown-glass icicles; when they're artistically frosted with acid, and water is dripping through the pinholes at the pointed ends, they look realer than real. And they don't melt under the hot lights.

These shops are only the beginning. Of course, if you're really interested in seeing how much and what varied work goes into the making of a picture, you can visit the glazier, a file shop, a pattern shop, and a big sandblasting shed where men clean rust and paint from all sorts of objects. The heavy planks which line its walls soon become smooth as driftwood, and are frequently used on beach sets for just that effect. And that's far from all.

Ed Willis' huge prop warehouse contains an upholstery shop, a drapery sewing room, a cabinet shop for making furniture, and an artificial flower shop. Again, only artificial flowers will hold their looks and shape under the merciless beating of Technicolor lights.

In Lou Kolb's electrical department there is a full-fledged foundry, a tin shop, machine shop, plating room, electrical repair division, welding shed, blacksmith shop, and an amazing precision-machine room for electronic and camera fittings where an ordinary watchmaker would seem as heavy handed as a sledge artist. When the director of *Ah, Wilderness!* demanded a brand-new Stanley steamer for Wallace Beery to drive proudly out of a salesroom, and the few antique models still available in the old car museums were too obviously antique, Kolb's metal workers turned out a custom job that Mr. Stanley could have been proud of. Practical, too, even though the puffing exhaust steam was actually ejected by a device originally built to blow smoke rings.

This reincarnated automobile had a further distinction; it was one of the few studio contraptions with which Jack Gaylord had nothing to do. Gaylord heads the collection of cottage crafts known collectively as prop shop. The shop makes anything, but Jack is the individual who usually figures how. A square-built and unassuming man with a tilted hat and tinted glasses (he nearly lost his eyes in a fog experiment), his wartime contributions included the pinboard method of making the relief maps which gave pilots a visualization of their air targets in a matter of hours rather than months.

Back in 1935, seeking a material for a mechanized tarpon which would "fight" the hook in *Captains Courageous,* he invented himself into a collaboration with Goodyear and helped develop what has since become famous as foam rub-

ber. (He claims that the new foamlike rubber now floating
in the Esther Williams tank is even better.)

But most of his work is the routine legerdemain of stag-
ing illusion, and his answers to complex prop problems are
usually ridiculously simple. To make the symbolic geranium
wilt as you watched it in *The Good Earth,* he merely injected water into the stem of a real geranium, kept it frozen
until the camera began to turn, then hit it with a beam of
infra-red heat.

And then there's mud. Real earth mud is heavy, settles
too quickly, and takes too long to put back "as was" for
repeated takes. So Jack's notes classify three assorted muds
as follows: "*Heavy,* to drive through; raw oatmeal and water, colored with burnt umber or dirt. *Thin;* cornstarch
and water, colored with burnt sugar. Mud to hit people
in the face should usually be made from chocolate." Most
fogs are atomized Nujol. To make the low clinging variety, for example, the Nujol is sprayed through a dry-ice
cooling-box out over wetted ground. Jack and the boys
put a good deal of time working the reality into the earthquakes of *San Francisco* and *Green Dolphin Street.* But
that mechanized tarpon turned out too real for its own
good, and probably for the health of the gullible shark
off Catalina who found himself suddenly trying to digest
$3000 worth of Gaylordian electrical apparatus.

It is hard to tell where Gaylord leaves off and the operating men pick up, men like Vic Millar and Walter Brown and
George Lofgren. But they are the last ones to worry about
it, because the inventing and making and operating are
often inextricably mixed up. Officially, these fellows operate all moving props, from mechanized bedbugs to the full-
sized practical train over on Lot 3, and they produce all

rain and snow and the other tangible changes in stage weather known as "effects."

Rain is real water, falling in drops of adjustable size and frequency from rain-heads on as many as thirty overhead pipe lines. The reason rain seldom photographs well in home cameras, by the way, is that it must be backlit, so that the rain falls between the camera and some sort of high-lighted background.

Snow has changed a lot over the last few years. The old reliable cornflakes are more or less out of favor, since what they do to dialogue when actors walk around on them shouldn't happen to a sound man. Ground-up chicken feathers make the most convincing fall, but they are apt to start "falling" upside down in the least little draft and they infest a stage forever after, like lint. We probably came closest to wintry reality in *Battleground*, which was as snowy a picture as you can get without starring penguins. In the first place, the entire enormous Stage 15 was kept very cold and damp so that the breath of the soldiers would show. Most of the snow on the background earth and in drifts was white gypsum plaster fresh from the bag. Close to camera and in contact with the actors, the snow was produced by Mr. Britt's secret formula so perfectly that it actually felt damp on the skin, slid off slick surfaces like rubber and clung to wool, and even tread down and crunched as the men walked on it. The blizzardy realism of ice projected from a shredder into the blast of a wind machine provided the material for the snowball sequence. But most of the falling snow was Foamite fire-extinguishing liquid which was shot out at the top of the stage from special atomizing blowers. This, incidentally, gave rise to one of those persistent minor problems of realism. The falling snow would naturally pile up on stones, tree branches, and other cold objects. But this Foamite snow also wanted to pile up on the men's helmets, where real snow would be melted by body heat. So the helmets were coated with chemicals to dissolve the Foamite back into its original liquid state—and the realistic "melting" which resulted was an unexpected bonus.

Just before a recent Christmas we sent a crew to a downtown hospital to shoot some scenes for the *March of Dimes* trailer. The cameraman couldn't get a satisfactory reflection of the patient's face in the tiny rear-view automobile mirror with which the iron lungs were equipped. So he sent out to the prop shop. The boys developed the special fittings for a big mirror which worked fine, but there was an unexpected aftermath. The patient was overjoyed with his new breadth of view almost to the point of tears, and the word of the new mirror spread to the other patients like wildfire. The result was that the boys in the shops worked all night for the two nights before Christmas on their own time to make up forty-eight of these mirrors (Gaylord typically added some ingenious clips on the reverse side to hold a magazine in reading position) and on Christmas morning each patient in the hospital was equipped.

Every foreman on the back lot figures that he has the best crew in the business. He seldom gives orders; the men know what is needed and go about it. As Vic Millar said, after completing one particularly rugged assignment, "The boys knew we'd all do it together or we'd all go down in a heap."

15

Monday, the Wellman company went out on location.

The Bennett company was on location in Africa, Potter in England, and the Saville second unit was on its way back from India. But we went to 4233 Lebourget Street, a half mile outside the studio fence.

Near or far, the Production Department shudders at all locations. They lose that tight control they have inside the studio and put themselves at the mercy of weather, bad light, volunteer actors who pop up from nowhere into the middle of scenes, and a fabulous variety of unwanted sound effects over the dialogue. On a single afternoon, mixer Connie Kahn encountered dogs, birds, cement mixers, telephone bells, loud radios, children fighting, the exhaust from a cleaner's shop, a lawnmower, and, one that had us mystified for an hour, a little boy with bells on his shoes.

But the weather was wonderful, the bright sun and cloudless sky which electricians call "grip weather," because most of the lighting is handled with shades and reflectors.

Nevertheless, the electricians clocked into the studio in the pre-dawn fog right along with the grips and prop men and the others. They loaded their clutter of equipment and rumbled away on the trucks about seven o'clock. The seventy extras and day players who would represent Joe Smith's neighbors formed a motley procession up the studio street to the buses and were on their way a little after

eight. When they reached the location they found the erstwhile quiet residential street already jammed with the characteristic assortment of vehicles: the big green stake-bodied
trucks from which the equipment was being unloaded, the
long black staff limousines, the crew buses, and such less
usual vehicles as spotless aluminum toilet trailers for extras
and crew, dressing-room trailers for the principals, a station wagon with the portable sound recorder, and the snack
wagon of an outside concessionaire.

Most of the real residents were standing in their door-
ways and in knots on the sidewalk watching the sights.
Probably they were somewhat relieved; a month ago when
two of the long black limousines had pulled up and a dozen
quiet men got out and stared intently at the houses, somebody had called the police.

Already, at eight-fifteen, set decorators had cleaned out
the "Smith" garage, a drapery man had hung the curtains
from Stage 18 in the Smith house front windows, a greens-
man had adjusted the shrubbery to match that on the stage,
and Wellman had put his first shot in the can, the "geography" long shot of Joe's house which opens the picture.
Much of Wellman's and Mellor's routine was the same as
you had seen inside the stage.

For others, working outdoors made quite a difference,
Joel had to boom his instructions for the background action over the portable electric megaphone. Philbrick's electricians had to lay long cables up the gutters from the
big green generator truck parked around the block out of
sound range (arcs use direct current, seldom available from
city lines, and lights are needed to provide the artificial
"fill" light which softens the contrasting shadows on the
side of actors' faces away from the sun). The grips had set

up foil-faced reflectors to bounce the sunlight in desired directions, and they would set up various kinds of diffusion and shade to soften the flat, sharp "newsreel" lighting of the sun when the camera went in close. Over in the station wagon, Connie Kahn and his recordist hugged earphones to their heads, fighting the constant succession of extraneous sounds. Regular city traffic policemen, working for us on their days off, were posted around the perimeter: they own their own uniforms, and we supply them with rented motorcycles which are painted in the official city black-and-white but bear private license plates.

At eight-twenty unit manager Ruby, his professional pessimism finally overcome, phoned the Production office to cancel out the cover-set arrangement which would have used these extras inside a studio stage had the weather crossed him up.

At eight-twenty-five Bill Wellman okayed the shot of Joe coming home from his day's work and turning on the lawn sprinklers; the early morning shadows still were long enough to photograph like late afternoon. While prop men dried off the sprinkled sidewalks with blow-torches, Mellor's men moved the camera back across the street to get the shot of Joe racing his car backward out of his driveway into a near collision. That went in on Take 1, and after a change of wardrobe we got the "reformed" slow back-out for the fourth day. Then Whitmore and young Gary gave way to the stunt drivers, and we got the scene on the second day where irritated Joe roars his car out of the driveway into the waiting arms of George Chandler, the motorcycle cop.

George, by the way, has worked in every Wellman picture since *A Star Is Born*, and when he signed on for this part a month ago he rented a motorcycle and had been learning to stunt it with the proper verve ever since. The scream now heard was from Chandler when he found that stunt rider Jack Semple was going to ride the near-miss, and Chandler would merely do the nice safe acting in the dialogue shots which followed.

The screams worked, because after the closeup where Joe got the ticket and raced out of the scene, Chandler got to turn on his siren and ride the pursuit in person.

Bill and the camera and the crew moved up the street, grabbing one setup after another, and by eleven-fifty-five they finished the very funny scenes between Joe and the cop and knocked off for lunch.

Lunch was the typical location layout. Trucks from Brittingham's had rolled in shortly before noon, and the caterer's men had set up long tables and benches. Wellman and the staff parked at a table over near the camera, where Mellor had commandeered a camera umbrella, to lay plans for the afternoon's work. But everybody else lined up for a lunch from the service tables and settled down for the hour break.

Ruby always tries to serve a hot-plate lunch, but the more usual box-lunches are really very good. You may tire of turkey sandwiches for a few days after Thanksgiving if Britts have over-figured for their restaurants, but the boxes contain two ample meat sandwiches, a boiled egg or two, an apple or orange, some cookies or cake, and a carton of ice cream. Milk or coffee at the counter. There is no limit on repeats, and some of the extras put away meals which could last them a couple of days, and probably do when extra work is no more plentiful than usual. The veteran extras picked out the shady spots on the grass of the little park, the youngsters were herded to their legally required rest in a rented patio down the street, and the crews began drifting over toward the next setup.

Joe spent the next hour and a half doing the two-minute walk across the park, the crew moving the camera along through a half-dozen setups to visualize the skeletal script instructions: "All the neighbors are out, watering lawns, digging, tinkering with their cars. . . . Joe exchanges friendly greetings with several of them." Now Joel's advance planning of the background action paid off. The youngsters were lackadaisical in their first two runs toward the Good Humor Truck, until the word went around that there was real ice cream in there for free and the blasé child extras suddenly turned into hungry kids. A bit man was to be washing a car in a driveway and Wellman let the company use his dusty convertible, didn't charge us a cent. There was no way of getting an overhead mike into the final conversation between Joe and Mr. Brannan without casting a boom shadow into the scene, so lanky Fred Faust crawled along behind the hedge with the microphone in his hand.

The next half hour, over in Joe's back yard, accounted for several tie-up shots; Joe and Johnny walking out to the garage on different days, starting the car backouts, and Mary at the window. When those were done it was late enough so that the long afternoon shadows began looking like the very early morning which we needed for the sequence of Joe sheepishly delivering his son's newspaper route.

The work had been going well all day, but now it accelerated. There's a wonderful atmosphere when a crew is keyed high and shooting fast: a take goes in, the key men swing in for a quick huddle around the director, take his instructions, and spread out again to jump for the new setup. The last bit went in just about twilight, boosted by every arc Philbrick could blast at it. Mellor had barely clicked off his test when the smog rolled in and the light was gone in five minutes.

To get a jump on that precious production time, the electricians sent word up the street to save some dinner for them, and went to work lighting up the houses for the night shots. Ordinary household lighting lets the windows seem dark on film, so the boys put 5 K Pans behind the visible windows of Joe's house and the homes on either side, planted floods behind some shrubbery to warm up the house fronts, and placed arcs in the back yards to give the houses some outline and depth. Location fixer Charlie Coleman, despite the emergency complaints he had been adjusting during the day, had made most of his neighborhood arrangements ahead of time. We paid $100 per shooting day rentals for Joe's house and the Brannan place, and $25 each to their neighbors. Mrs. Catlan, the schoolteacher who owns Joe Smith's house, said it felt very odd to stand out on the street behind the camera and watch other people apparently living in her home.

After dinner, with the big Brutes blazing blue-white from their towers and half the town gathered around to see the show, Wellman checked off all the neighborhood night shots. Joe's bowling partners dropped him off in front of his house and said good night via the mike in the car's glove compartment, Joe and Mary went out to their car and started for the hospital and the false labor, and finally Joe walked up on Brannan's porch and found that his runaway son was inside. The high arcs clanked off and the streets grew dark and the crowd began to melt away.

The day's work had netted the really phenomenal total of twenty-five completed scenes, in forty-seven separate and distinct camera setups. The 745 feet of actual screen footage would run eight and a quarter minutes! Wellman was driving this picture through as he used to drive the silents. Out of the 168 scenes in the script, he now had shot 107. And we were six days ahead of what we had thought an impossibly fast schedule. The gamble was looking better.

The staff hurried back to the studio to check out their paper-work. The grips wrestled in their platforms, brackets, and camera tracks. The electricians pulled their miles of writhing cables out of dark gutters and back yards, and one by one the trucks rumbled their exhausts and rolled out past the park up to the boulevard. It had been a sixteen-hour day of rugged labor, but they could loll in bed until six o'clock tomorrow morning. It was close to midnight when the laborer policed up the last paper cup and blackened flashlight bulb.

Not until the next day would a hundred-odd people realize that they were suffering not from some strange skin disease, but that their long day in the open had sunburned their scalps clear down through their hair. Charlie Coleman took a last look around, crossed his fingers, and the maintenance pickup jounced away up the sleeping street.

16

Mary Smith was originally going to have her baby on Stage 18, but a man named Joe Cooke switched her to 19 to make room for a cocktail lounge. This sort of thing happens every noon, when Fred Gabourie walks down from his Construction Department after lunch and meets assistant production manager Cooke for their daily session of set-spotting.

The set-spotting room is up in the Art Department. Its principal furnishing is a big rack of plotting boards, one for each of the stages, which map the size and position of doors, sunken pits, power connections, and other items of interest. Scraps of transparent tracing paper thumb-tacked to the boards show the exact position on the stage floors of sets now standing. Waiting for Joe Cooke is a bundle of new tracings, representing sets which directors expect to start using within the next week, and these are the sets for which he must find a spot.

Since no Art Director willingly consents to strike a set until dry rot begins to set in (he's right to keep it standing as long as there's a chance of re-takes or added scenes), stage space is always at a premium. M-G-M's stage numbers run up to 30, but Joe and Gabe actually have twenty-three stages to work with. Some of the stages are allotted to other uses, such as storage and set assembly. Others are adapted to special purposes; No.1 for music recordings, No.2 for sound and dialogue recordings, 5 and 6 for theatre and opera-house sets, 12 for rear-projection process, 14 for miniature work, and 30 for scenes which need its 800,000 gallon concrete tank. The working stages sometimes get pretty crowded, but Joe "puzzles the stuff in somehow."

Joe's recurrent nightmare is that he will schedule two different companies to shoot on the same stage on the same day. He therefore likes to allot whole stages to just one company where possible, and so most of the *Next Voice* interiors were assembled on Stages 18 and 19.

Six major sets were puzzled onto the floor of 18; the whole Joe Smith home, the aircraft locker room, Joe's garage, the cocktail lounge, the saloon, and the interior of a drug store for the montage. With another fifteen feet Cooke could have puzzled in the montage hamburger stand. While this looked at first glance like the most cluttered maze a man could devise, actually the sets had been cunningly angled so there was plenty of room for each camera angle which Eddie Imazu had indicated on the tracings.

Realistic though these sets looked, from the camera side, they cost less than you might think. For example, take the complete Joe Smith house of living room, dining room, kitchen, hallway and two bedrooms, with a finished exterior front and enough lawn and painted scenic backing outside to let the camera shoot out through the windows on day scenes. Although it was built new, without stock units, it cost less than $5500 and we played sixty-six scenes in it. The locker room and each of the bar sets cost around $1000 each. We spent $8500 on the church interior, but the pictorial and plot climaxes took place there and justified the expenditure.

Every once in a while I find myself looking at a seemingly

ordinary set and realizing all over again a startling fact:
that every single object and item and detail is there only
because somebody thought of it ahead of time. The garage
attached to my house or yours has sort of "accumulated"
over the years. But the construction people and set decorators must start with nothing but the bare words: "INT.
JOE SMITH GARAGE—DAY" and use their creative imagina-
tions to realize that a pane of glass would have been broken
and patched with adhesive tape, that years of pressing
hands would have worn the paint on the side of the door,
and that young Johnny's outgrown baby buggy and tri-
cycle would have been put out here for storage along with
the half-emptied cans of paint, the paintbrushes left to soak,
the broken chair that Joe keeps meaning to fix and two
truckloads of other familiar paraphernalia. Work like this
is worth a closer look.

It's the day after the location. The company is back on
interiors, working on Stage 19 where Cooke has spotted
the hospital corridor and waiting room, along with the
church interior and the exterior of Brannan's back yard.

The awesome red light and buzzer hold us out on the
street for a moment, but they fade and we push inside through the heavy icebox doors of the sound-lock
vestibule. You breathe in that characteristic smell of the
sound stage: a blend of new paint, sawdust, cigarette smoke,
perfume, distant coffee, ozone from the arc lights and what
not else. Your view is blocked by the near rear wall of the
Brannan set, but the familiar pool of blue-white light is
welling up beyond it.

The sound of hammering and a mix of voices seem to
be filtering dimly, as from a great distance. The quilted
sound insulation which lines the walls and roof of the stage

kills all the normal bounce of the sound waves. Sound travels to the walls but sinks to its death in the absorbent quilting, giving you the strange feeling that your words evaporate into nothingness before they reach the ear of the person to whom you're talking. Most of the set walls, rigid though they look, are also sound-absorbent.

As you've seen earlier, practically all sets are built of prefabricated units. Our standard wall unit is a wooden frame: its bones show in the back, but over the front is stretched first a layer of black "daisy cloth" to block leakage of back light, over it goes a layer of unbleached muslin to keep the black from choking through to the camera, and finally the top finish which gets photographed is usually a layer of tightly stretched canvas, painted to specification. If the set is to show carved paneling, or stonework or brick, the same square frame can be fronted with the appropriate molded plaster or plastic facsimile. An added mixture of sawdust in the finished paint gives a canvas wall a perfect illusion of roughed plaster or adobe.

You may wonder about the rather frequent offsets in the walls of the sets: they're attractive, and they cast useful depth-creating shadows, but their real purpose is to conceal the joints between wall units. The units are nailed to each other, and held vertical and rigid by diagonal braces to the stage floor and to the lighting scaffolds overhead. Interior sets seldom have ceilings, because so much of the light must be fed down into the scene from above. Usually the camera is close enough to the characters so that your eyes never get up to ceiling height, but in the occasional long shot where the ceiling must become visible, it is usually managed by unrolling a sort of horizontal canvas curtain for the necessary distance. Most doors and windows

are "practical"—industry jargon meaning that a thing really
works—and are solidly constructed so that a character can
leave a scene without seeming to shake his house down
behind him. Naturally we build only as much set as is necessary for the action to be played in it, and that's the reason
you will often see just a corner of a room or a piece of wall
with a door in it or a façade which ends halfway up the
second story.

Near the big main door of the stage, where they can
be hauled out easily when the company moves elsewhere,
are the portable dressing-rooms for the leading players.
Square, shiny, one-room trailer affairs which are hauled
around from stage to stage by bustling little tractors, they
are very cheerful little places, and the steps leading up
into the bright interiors give them the air of an odd little
residential street. Democratically adjacent are the knock-
down dressing-rooms built of black flats for the minor
players. Just beyond is a row of battered green make-up
tables, rows of bare bulbs rimming their aged mirrors, and
long canvas-covered benches for the extras.

Most of the extras have been around the business for
some time, and are no longer impressed by what once they
might have thought glamorous. When they're not working
they sit about alone and in groups talking, knitting, playing cards, dozing, reading *Variety* and *The Hollywood Reporter*, even occasionally standing on the set to look at the
principals in action. Middle-aged moviegoers can usually
spot some once-familiar faces among the atmosphere players,
and when you hear a bit line such as, "Watch where you're
going, mister!" you're often hearing a person who once
earned several thousand dollars a week and now is grateful

for the chance to speak the single line which boosts the $15.56 extra's check to a bit player's $55.00.

Extras, by the way, are always telephoning, mostly to see whether Central Casting has something for them tomorrow: there is always someone in the phone booths outside the stages and a line of others awaiting their turn. Studio commissaries all over town give extras their lunch change in nickels and dimes. A mysterious phrase you're sure to hear floating from that booth is, "But nothing close, dear." The extra is reporting to Central that she worked in a scene but not close enough to camera to be recognized again by the audience. Only the new and ambitious extras push forward to get their faces in the camera; the old hands gladly pass up the glory in exchange for the additional days of work.

Here on 19, the lights are on in the long hospital corridor set, but things are oddly quiet; the camera position is deserted, and the only person working is Jimmy Luttrell as he polishes footprints from the shiny linoleum floor. Some sort of problem has come up and we're waiting while somebody goes to get something: the technicians will give you a much more detailed explanation, but mine is simpler and just as enlightening. Probably it's something about the corridor.

Everybody hates to work in corridors. They're long and narrow sets, of course, closed in on both sides, and the director usually wants his characters to walk all the way down the distance, whispering to each other. The lighting must be high and uniform all the way rather than concentrated in "positions," almost as rugged as bringing a star down one of those long curving state staircases.

The sound men could mount a mike on the camera if this were a travel shot, but Wellman wants the effect of the small figures growing large as they approach his standing camera. There is no possibility of using a moving microphone boom, so Fred Faust must tie his mike to a "fishpole" and walk along the high scaffolding as the actors move along the corridor below him, fish-poling the mike down between the lights and crossbeams the best he can. Probably that's the cause of the delay; mixer Kahn has called Sound to send down one or two more men to work the scaffold route in relays.

Bill Wellman has walked off the set and is back in a canvas chair going through his usual between-takes routine. Secretary Ethel Eickhoff has brought down the paper-work from his office and he's trying to dictate in snatches. Leonard Murphy from Casting is escorting two elderly women for Bill to choose between for the "woman in awe" in the church scene. Bill looks at the two nice old ladies as they try to conceal their nervous eagerness and says, "How can a man choose between two such beautiful creatures? We'll use *two* women in awe." Eddie Imazu is holding the model of the Brannans' back yard set and wants an okay on some changes. Wardrobe waits its chance to get an approval on the spinsterish hat which actress Lillian Bronson will wear in the church scene. Publicity's Jim Merrick has a Distinguished Visitor in tow and still-man Eddie Hubbell waits his chance to bang off a flashbulb on a shot of the visitor with Bill. The still-man replies to Bill's objection with a cheerful, "Go ahead and fire me, I still got that little pony in my back yard." Bill poses, with a gracious smile. Joel comes in with his, "Okay, Mr. Wellman, we're ready." And Bill's little between-takes relaxation comes to an end.

Bill tries a run-through, and the scene begins to come up. At the far end of the corridor, Mary comes out of the door wearing her coat and carrying her bag, smiles at anxious Joe and says with embarrassment as they walk up the corridor, "See what you married? I'm just a false alarm." Joe takes her bag, grins his reassurance, and as they come close to camera Mary says, "I feel like such a fool—leaving here just as big as when I came in," and they walk off camera. Bill calls over his shoulder, "How is it now, Marconi?" and Kahn walks in from his panel.

Visitors often slip the mixer's headphones over their ears, and immediately yank them away as though they were exploding. That sensitive mike at the end of the boom seems to be picking up everything for miles around in a screaming jumble and jangling roar from which it seems impossible that intelligible dialogue could ever emerge. The reason is simple enough: nature has given human ears and brains the power of selectivity, enabling us to tune out or ignore unwanted sounds to such an extent that a dozen couples can carry on individual conversations all at once in the same room. But the tin ear of the mike picks up all sounds, without selection, in an indiscriminate hodge-podge which sound men call "mike stew."

This time, Kahn figured that all would be well if Mary would delay her last line just a little longer, until she would be directly under his last overhead mike. Bill agreed, the grips chalked Mary's new position on the floor, and the shot went in on Take 1. Just for protection, Kahn had Mary stand still directly under a close mike and record both lines "wild," without camera.

Bill moved in for the pickup shots, which ran off rapidly. Joel called out the time-honored gag which signals a move-over—"We're in the wrong set, boys," and the crew began swinging the setup toward the adjacent church interior.

Joe Cooke strode out from behind the far end of the corridor. If the wild flat behind the delivery-room doors was moved back against the wall, there would be twenty feet of beautiful empty floor space. The montage hamburger stand would be in there tomorrow.

17

The lighted streets which we see over Mary's shoulder as she and Joe drive to the hospital were actually photographed while she was having her baby on Stage 19. This spectral sort of accomplishment is the routine work of a ghost director named Johnny Waters, who is in charge of the Second Unit. A big ruddy Irishman with a smooth mop of white hair and a rich New York accent, Johnny has seen about everything there is to see in the picture business and throws his cues with equanimity from a racing camera car, a swaying dredge bucket, a diving plane or a bobbing pontoon raft.

The Second Unit of a company, in general, picks up outdoor shots in which the principals either do not appear, or work sufficiently far away from camera to permit doubling. In between his four calls on *Next Voice* Johnny Waters handled, as typical assignments, an automobile race for Gable's *To Please a Lady* and the hilarious Hyster and speedboat chase stuff for Skelton's *Watch the Birdie*. His assignment for this particular March evening was to get a shot of the *Next Voice* motorcycle officer leading Joe's old car through the night traffic and into the hospital ambulance entrance, plus some background plates of the same ride as viewed through what would later seem to be the windows of Joe's moving car.

The last reds were fading from the sunset as the studio cars pulled up at the location curb. Already parked were

the grip trucks, the four "picture cars," the local traffic
policemen, and the camera car. Maybe it's because it goes
back to the romantic early days of movies when cameramen
turned their caps around backwards as they cranked their
tripod cameras, but there is still something very glamorous
to me about a camera car.

For tonight's trip the "flying bridge" top platform
carried two big sun-arcs on swivel mountings, fed by a
three-hundred-ampere gas generator behind the cab. Short,
cheerful Hal Lipstein and his crew began mounting their
silent cameras on an aluminum beam across the rear platform, and director Waters began laying out the first deal.
The city had promised to turn on the street lamps a half
hour early, to give him the effect of night while there was
still enough afterglow light to lend definition to the buildings and cars.

The first shot was to show the motorcycle officer leading
Joe's car down the street, across a busy intersection, and
into the hospital yard. The prop man set up a sign "Ambulance Entrance," the assistant director stationed the cars
which would swing out of the lanes to let Joe roll through,
and the city traffic officers got ready to block "civilian"
traffic on Johnny's signal. The dusk began to settle, but
the street lights didn't come on. The watches still lacked
five minutes of the agreed time, but the ideal conditions
for this type of shot fade so fast that there is always an
urgency in the crew; to the cameraman it's time, tide, and
light that wait for no man. Then suddenly the street lamps
came on, in a beautiful glow, right to the second.

Johnny ran a final check of his arrangements. The elements of the scene were spread over several city blocks,
where a walkie-talkie radio rig would have saved invaluable

time, but the signals came back okay. The two cameras
were set to crank at eighteen frames per second, so as to
increase the apparent speed of the cars when the print
clicked through theatre projectors at the standard speed
of twenty-four. The two pedestrian atmosphere extras
would do their walk in a sort of slow motion, to look normal later on. Johnny blew the whistle to get set, the traffic
officers set up their blocks, and the streets went suddenly
empty. Johnny flashed the agreed cue on the arcs.

Far down the street the four atmosphere cars pulled out
from the curb and went into motion. The camera car
ground into gear and started accelerating, with the motorcycle and Joe's car roaring along behind, outlined in the
vague blue-white of the shuttered arcs. Sirens wailing and
motors roaring, the crew hanging onto the rail, the three
cars flashed past the extra cars one by one, and neared the
intersection, hoping that no volunteers had strayed through
the traffic blocks. The camera car hit the car tracks, swung
sharp left and stopped, to let Lippy's camera fast-pan the
cycle and Joe's car across the intersection past the "Ambulance Entrance" sign into the hospital yard. In another two
minutes the light was gone; hot or cold, that was it. Johnny
threw the signal to unblock the civilian traffic and head
for the next setup.

The script clerk scrawled on his log, "WX 160 A-BACK-
GROUND PLATE Joe's Car, Night" and the crew repeated the
same run, except as though looking back out of Joe's car.

You're entitled to ask at this point, "What is a background plate?" I think you are entitled to a frank answer.
There has always been a sort of iron curtain in the industry
around some of its most fascinating and ingenious work.

We are not supposed to tamper with the audience's illusion that whatever they see on the screen actually happened just that way. But I doubt if any audience believes M-G-M had cameramen at the San Francisco earthquake, or that we were able to send our representatives back almost twenty centuries in time to film the actual burning of Rome. I am very proud of some of the extraordinarily inventive and ingenious things the industry can do, and I see no valid reason for keeping them under cover.

It's obvious that even with all our resources of set construction and location shooting, some essential shots are just plain impractical. For an everyday example, when you see Joe and Mary on the way to the hospital you want to look into their faces close up to find out how they feel about what's happening. But the mechanical problems of mounting a camera on the hood of the moving car, lighting the faces and recording intelligible sound would run up the cost to a point where we couldn't give you the scene.

And many of the most memorable scenes in the history of movies are downright "impossibles." These are the San Francisco earthquakes, the bombings of Tokyo, the burnings of Atlanta, the sinkings of the *Titanics*, the train wrecks and the oil-well fires and the automobile crashes and atomic-bomb explosions, and so on through the gamut of pictorial and dramatic spectacle. These are things that audiences want to see. Many a wonderful story can be brought to the screen only if the spectacular event which climaxes its action can somehow be recreated.

And so, all through the industry, the answer to the impractical and the impossible comes from a little group of specialists whom outsiders regard as the Magic Department.

Most people have heard by now about rear projection process. Most of our process work is done on Stage 12, and it was to that stage on an afternoon late in the schedule that the Wellman company put the human action in front of Johnny Waters' background plates.

The interior of the big bare stage was painted soot-black, to kill any reflections of light as dead as the quilted insulation kills the sound waves. Down toward one end of the stage stood a large framework in which was suspended, by a sort of tennis-racket lacing, a transparent movie screen of pearly plastic. It was about twelve feet square. At the other end of the stage a caboose-like projection booth was mounted in a sort of portable elevator. On Wellman's signal, its projector would beam background traffic scene WX-160A onto the rear of the transparent screen, recreating the second journey which Johnny Waters had shot looking backwards as though from Joe's car.

On a platform in front of this transparent screen, hence also in front of the flickering traffic scene, was mounted an exact duplicate of Joe's beat-up old car, sawed off at the windshield so that you had a full view of Joe sitting behind the wheel and Mary beside him. The actors were lit very carefully so that no light could leak onto the background screen.

The camera stood in front of the platform looking into the open-faced car, and through the car to the screen behind it. It was a standard sound camera except that its shutter was synchronized to open and close exactly in step with that of the rear projector. And as the strip of film went through this camera it photographed Joe and Mary, plus the moving street and traffic background which was visible through the car's rear window on the process screen.

There was a good deal of thought and skill involved in this operation, even apart from the ability of the process crew to match the lighting of the two elements so that they would seem to have been photographed simultaneously on the original location.

The cut-up car body was mounted on springs. Effects operators jiggled it slightly for the illusion of motion, and tilted it on the turns. Just below Joe's feet, a man turned a crank at the base of the steering column in synchronization with the picture so that Joe would seem to turn the steering wheel as the background turned. Wellman protected the illusion with such cautions as, "Joe, look toward the left before you turn your wheel that way," and, "Remember, in a noisy car you'd have to push your voices a little." And Waters had protected Wellman by shooting the same plates three ways: straight back, angling left, and angling right, so that Bill could take his choice of closeup angles on his actors.

As you see, this is an honest illusion. It merely brings two separated pieces of reality into a new combination. Audiences want the satisfaction of seeing authentic backgrounds, so science brings the mountain in through the main gate to where Mahomet waits, made up and ready to go. Any dialogue scene in a moving vehicle is most likely a process shot if you see scenery moving past the window, although on poverty budgets a director is prone to switch the scene to night and have some of the boys run past the window waving flashlights. Come to think of it, there was a man on Stage 12 flashing a Junior across Joe and Mary to simulate the passing traffic.

Back on Stage 18, you may have noticed another kind of illusion background. Or, like a certain visitor, you may not have noticed it. Looking out through the front window of Joe Smith's living room he expressed his concern that we would go to the expense of building a whole grassy park, dozens of trees, and twenty or thirty houses inside a stage. He felt rather sheepish a moment later when he found that he had been looking at one of George Gibson's scenic backings, a continuous canvas background so cleverly painted to reproduce the actual Joe Smith location street that it took hold of his eye and carried it right out to the horizon line.

The *Next Voice* backings were comparatively small, and their only function was to protect Wellman if he wanted to angle a daytime shot so that the camera must look through a window in the background. But Gibson's beautiful backing for the Concord street in *Little Women* was 600 feet long, covering three walls of enormous Stage 15, and sixty feet high. It blended with the actual set buildings in the foreground and carried the scene back over fields and woods and rolling hills to a horizon which photographed as miles distant. And in Technicolor. In no other way could we give audiences the beauty and scope of that scene and the authentic look of the New England countryside, and yet be able to photograph the same set with the snow and rain and dry grass and autumn leaves of all four seasons within the few weeks' span of a shooting schedule.

Gibson's workshop is the oddly tall, thin building ("a two-story building ten stories high") which towers above the rest of the back lot. The floor on which the artists work is fifty feet above ground level. The roof is fifty feet higher than that, and the canvases in work hang from

frames which move up and down past the artists on eleva-
tors. Scenic artists trained in the theatre have a considerable
adjustment to make out here; where a theatre stage set
can be impressionistic, movie backings must seem to be
the acme of realism. Strangely, however, photo-murals
(enormously enlarged actual photographs) aren't very
successful. Our artists must constantly "force" their true
perspectives and values and colors to get the illusion of
depth. Like the cameraman and gaffer, Gibson is always
fighting for separations, to pull foreground objects out from
the background. But he must do it on several levels with
only a single flat surface to work with.

Since this handcraft art must be produced on a production-line basis—murals by the acre—Scotch-burred Gibson has developed a number of ingenious shortcuts. His
men use stencils for painting in the brickwork or clap-
boards of large walls. The wholesale foliage of a distant
woods goes on with an ordinary brush which has been
partly "filled" with shellac so that the wetted bristles separate into a hundred clumps, like the fur of a soaked cat.
It used to be a slow and expensive job to paint the bark of
scores of trees, and to brush in each individual blade of
grass in a foreground field. But now a piece of carved felt
wrapped around a coffee can is dipped in paint and rolled
down the tree trunk to make bark, and an old brush handle
studded with a dozen ordinary pipe-cleaners will lay in
twelve realistically irregular blades of grass at one swoop
of an artist's arm.

When an art director needs just a fractional background,
or must have his reality cut up and put back together in a
more useful combination, he calls on the specialized talents

of a tall, inventive, chain-smoldering chess enthusiast named Warren Newcombe.

Much of Newcombe's work is a sort of college version of the old "glass shot," where the camera lens viewed the human action on a small actual set through a small piece of glass on which had been painted the much larger set which the director wished he had. This was very convenient for converting a few square feet of flagstone into INT. CATHEDRAL NOTRE DAME, but today's audiences wouldn't accept it as convincing.

A few weeks ago Art Director Dan Cathcart was working out a street scene for *Toast of New Orleans*. It was a short scene, but there was no street set on Lot 3 which had the distant background required by the plot. And he couldn't afford to build such an extensive layout. So he selected a Lot 3 street which could be inexpensively altered to suit up to the level of the first floor. Then on the day of shooting, Newcombe's cameraman Mark Davis photographed the action with the upper part of his lens blocked off (with a matte), thus leaving his film unexposed above that first-floor level. Then the Newcombe artists went to work on the upper half. Working in the top portion of a 22″x28″ canvas, an architectural draftsman laid in the outline of the typical lacy New Orleans ironwork on the balconies in the foreground, completed the upper portions of the buildings along the street, and outlined the imaginary rooftops and steeples in the distance which Cathcart had sketched. The color artist completed the work.

After some extraordinarily careful testing, the half-exposed film of the street scene was loaded into the Newcombe camera. The matte was now reversed to block off the bottom part of the lens, and the exposure of the film was completed with this beautifully detailed miniature painting. The boys tricked some moving smoke and foliage into the shot, but that was sheer virtuosity.

The use of this matte-and-painting technique permits us to add a good deal of beauty and scope which picture budgets couldn't otherwise afford. Shooting under the economical controlled conditions on our stages and on back-lot sets, or on accessible locations, we can call on Newcombe to change the background of a summer home from the existing oil wells to a storied sea (*The Happy Years*), put a mountainous landscape behind a flat-land village (*Crisis*), or build the city of Rome on a shot of barren hills. On his repair shift, Newcombe can remove telephone poles from the background of a medieval village, add the plotted storm clouds to an as-shot cerulean sky, and supply the lighted windows for a day-for-night scene which was shot in the economical daylight with camera filters.

When Sam Wood was making *The Stratton Story*, a certain background plate of a double-decked baseball park was ideal except that it showed a scabrous patch of empty seats right in the middle of the upper tier. So Newcombe's group performed a skin-grafting operation, and if you were to examine the frames of the final picture under a microscope you would find a little group of spectators getting double value for its money, sitting in the lower and upper tiers simultaneously. But probably the loveliest of his recent jobs is in the scene of *Annie Get Your Gun* where Betty Hutton and Howard Keel stand on the swaying platform of an old-fashioned train and sing "Falling in Love is Wonderful"—as the Newcombe landscape behind them moves and changes and the sun sets tint by tint in glorious Technicolor

Not all impractical scenes are impractical because of cost or time or distance. Almost every story has some segment which, though essential to a rounded telling, threatens to stretch out to an impractically long footage, or to become dull. These problems usually end up in the bungalow of round-faced, earnestly intent Peter Ballbusch, whose specialty is montage.

Montage has been called the shorthand of the movies. It's cinema in its pure form, an impressionistic composite of image and movement and visual rhythm. It uses all the tricks, the zooms and cross-dissolves and superimposures of related objects, to make its plot points crystal clear in an amazingly short time. There is a tendency to misuse montage as a sort of special act, setting it off from the flow of the film with signaling dissolves and music. And so I was particularly pleased that the montage in *Next Voice* where Joe roves the night streets, looking for his son, is never spotted as such.

Whether recognized or not, montage is probably as useful a tool as we have in the whole cinema kit. In a matter of seconds, it lets us cover long time-lapses in a story, show the "progress" of a journey or a rise to fame or a battle, depict a whole phase of a man's life, arouse an emotion or create a mood or establish an atmosphere, summarize the pressures which cause the change in a character's mind, intensify the excitement of an earthquake or similar spectacular event, report the stream-of-consciousness turmoil inside a mind, depict a dream, and so on and on. But Ballbusch often gets his assignment after the sneak preview, when montage is called upon to plug a hole in the story, to condense a series of scenes which miss fire with the audience, or perhaps just to help shorten a too-long picture down to a feasible running time. But whatever the objective, the germ essence of a montage effect is a cleverly guided association of ideas in the audience's mind (hence the frequent superimposures), and the essential device is juxtaposition.

Juxtaposition, in the movie sense, means that any two pieces of film, when placed next to each other, combine into a new concept which neither of the pictures had by itself. I'll want to talk about this later when we look into editing and cutting, but Slavko Vorkapitch, who was in charge of montage at the studio for many years, put it this way: "When an American Indian wants to tell another from a different tribe that he is happy, he makes signs for 'Sunrise—in the Heart.' He puts together two apparently unrelated images and lo, an expression visual and rich is born —a perfect montage."

Out of montage has come the symbolism of the American movie, a language as individual and vivid and changing as slang. We see the funnel of an ocean liner and the wake of a steamer and we know that our hero has crossed the ocean. A glimpse of radio towers tells us that the news is going out. The spinning wheels of a train, the quaking of earth and a toppling wall, the banging gavel of a judge, a hundred or a thousand other symbolic images condense minutes of meaning into seconds of film time.

These earthquakes we've been hearing about, as well as the ship sinkings, airplane battles, dinosaur fights, circustent fires, munitions ship explosions, and other such "impossibles" fall mostly in the province of the studio's specialist in cosmic catastrophe, pipe-chewing Buddy Gillespie of the Art Department.

Buddy has been here since 1923, a year longer than newcomers Newcombe and Irving Ries. Although he has charge of all rear-projection process work, and also of full-scale effects such as burning down houses or toppling a wall on Gable, his most interesting work is done in miniature. The word "miniature" is misleading, however, because the Rome which he helped Nero to burn contained several hundred complete buildings on two acres of ground, and the jungle trees which he felled for *Green Dolphin Street* were fifteen feet high.

Miniature work is seldom used to save money. In fact, Warner Brothers are said to have spent $800,000 for the miniature work of a single picture, *Air Force*. Obviously, the director on a *Wizard of Oz* cannot very well send out a nine A.M. call for a real tornado, nor instruct it to try an entrance more to the left on the next take. So, like the work in the other Effects Departments, miniatures are mostly used to satisfy the audience' desire for spectacle and sweeping action that cannot in any other way be brought to their eyes.

An example is the avalanche in *Kim*. An essential plot point requires Kim to dislodge one small rock at the top of a mountain, the rock bouncing down and dislodging others until half the mountainside seems to give way in a thundering granite fury which buries Kim's pursuers. We tried to get this shot on a real mountain in full scale, up near Mt. Whitney. Even though we nearly buried the camera crew, the important action happened so far from the camera and was so widely dispersed that it looked utterly unreal on the screen.

So Gillespie's men erected a rig over on Lot 3 which became known on the schedules as EXTERIOR, AVALANCHE.

It looked something like a baseball grandstand in general contour, forty feet across and fifty feet high at the rear, faced with a plank floor built on a 45° slope. This slanting floor was made up of many wooden trapdoors, each hinged so that it could swing up and out horizontally, and each supported by collapsible crutches called "weak-knees." The avalanche was rigged by loading all these horizontal gates with real boulders and gravel, interspersed here and there with gnarled juniper branches for trees and other bits of vegetation. When you looked up at it from Max Fabian's camera shelter at the bottom and let yourself go out of focus a little it was a completely real mountainside.

When the day came for the shot, Don Jahraus made his last check of the complicated layout and Carrol Shepphird rehearsed the operators for the last time. Then the last okay came down to Buddy. He took a final look around, crossed his fingers, and threw the cue. From the painted plaster crags far up at the top, one small stone came adrift, sending up little puffs of dust as it began to bounce down the slope. Other stones joined it and began to roll. Then the operators on the high control platform at the side began pushing the buttons which yanked the weak-knees out from under the horizontal gates, one by one, starting from the top in that downward progression which the plotted avalanche required. As gate after gate slammed down, its load of boulders joined the rolling slide until the last gates fell and the avalanche reached its thundering climax. When the dust settled and we looked up, our beautiful mountainside had changed back, Cinderella-like, into a sloping plank floor. But the avalanche was in the cameras, and it was wonderful. The rig had taken weeks to build, days to load and prepare. The avalanche went on film in forty seconds, and now the boys would have to re-load the whole thing to get the detail and pickup jobs and angles with which the cutter would build up the thrill and suspense.

The prop shop craftsmen can supply Gillespie with amazingly accurate miniatures. They have to be extraordinarily accurate, because of the fantastic magnification on the screen. So Buddy seldom worries about the appearance of his miniatures; his usual problem is how to bring their movements down to scale. The wrecked cars of a miniature freight train, for example, will turn over faster and tend to bounce higher than their full-scale counterparts. This problem becomes really serious on the "wet shots," since no one has yet discovered how to construct a small-scale drop of water.

However, Buddy has licked the other water problem— that of inducing small-scale waves and swells, complete with whitecaps and foam—by doping the water with one of the new chemical detergents to reduce the surface tension. And down under the waterline of his fifty-one foot ocean liner is a maze of pipe outlets through which compressed air activates the convincingly foamy bow wave and wake as the ship moves slowly across the Lot 3 tank. This tank is a concrete-floored ocean, 300 feet square and three feet deep overall with deeper pits for sinkings, and is backed by a painted canvas "sky" background which is taller and broader than most six-story buildings.

As this locale implies, practically all miniature work is filmed outdoors. Gillespie has found that he can best slow the movements of most miniatures down to scale by fast-cranking the cameras. In full size, this would obviously be slow-motion; in miniatures it looks just right. Since fast-cranking demands more light than stages can supply, miniature magic looks to the sun.

Sooner or later, most of the magic passes through the skilled and inventive hands of rotund Irving Ries and his department of Special Optical Effects.

"Opticals" include the routine fades and dissolves which punctuate all pictures and give them tempo and timing, but Ries's men go far beyond this kindergarten work. They are the technicians who made Gene Kelly dance hand in hand with the cartoon king, who perambulated the Canterville Ghost through solid walls, and who made possible the amazing ballet of shoes which apparently danced by themselves behind Fred Astaire in *The Barkleys of Broadway*.

Perhaps bored with elementary split-screen work, Ries has recently done a triple-split. It's in the *Watch the Birdie* camera shop, and Red Skelton plays himself, his father and his grandfather all at once in the same scene, probably the first time in Hollywood that one actor has had three stand-ins. Red sent up a memo that he wanted three checks on this picture, and periodically complained about the old ham of a grandfather who was stealing his scenes.

Much of Ries's work is handled by an amazing precision instrument called the optical printer. It looks rather like a very fancy lathe. One end is a miniature "projector" through which runs the film to be altered, and on the other end is a camera which can move in and out on a track, and tilt, so as to rephotograph any desired *part* of the original film. Such as that patch of spectators who moved upstairs in the *Stratton* grandstand. The optical printer often saves a situation by enlarging a selected fraction of an original long shot to get needed full-screen closeups which were missed during the schedule, or perhaps to build up the part of a newcomer whose appeal wasn't recognized until after the preview. The International Department depends on Ries to move in on an original scene so as to eliminate the marginal liquor bottles which would bar the foreign print from Pakistan, the winged angel which would bar it from Britain, and the "cleavage" which excites disapproval in everyone but audiences. Not long ago Mr. Ries personally caught a 222-pound marlin off Catalina and had a picture taken to prove it—but everybody in the industry professes to believe that he printed a stock fish into a back yard snapshot.

Ries's department is part of a larger organization through which everything has to go before it can reach an audience, John Nickolaus' film laboratory

The windowless concrete walls of the lab enclose some of the most bizarre sights of a bizarre business. In one room the white and chrome of ingenious machines whir silently in a dim greenish glow. In another, shadowy shapes glide silently about like gnomes in a Satanic red fog. Miles of shining wet film loop between ceilings and long swashing tanks in dim tiled caverns, and technicians tell you that although a million feet of film a day often move through here, thousands of gallons of chemical fluids are successfully kept within .1 degree of a constant temperature, and many kilowatts of electricity held within .2 of a volt. These are exacting standards, but necessary for quality, because of those twenty-four separate pictures which will pass through the theatre projector every second; each must match its mate in the scene, and match the same scene in hundreds of other prints. These controls explain why, they tell you, no longer is a certain scene sunny at the Bijou and gloomy at the Strand, and no longer need be feared the glaring contrast which loses the black buttons on the hero's dark suit.

The man who presides over this plant, which he himself designed and built after he came to the studio with Mr. Mayer twenty-five years ago, refuses to admit that this network of rubber piping, stainless steel tanks, and electronically controlled precision machinery is any more complex, in principle, than a hobbyist's home darkroom down by the furnace. "You folks snap a picture, develop the negative, and show the print to your friends," says Nickolaus, "and that's all we do here, except we do it continuously."

Nick permits himself to get excited about only one phase of his operation. He brags that he runs the cleanest place in the world. Literally that; when Nick says "dirty," he has in mind something like the squalor of a hospital operating room. "The most expensive thing we make is air," he explains. When the picture on the film is magnified 60,000 times on the screen of the Radio City Music Hall, "a tiny speck of dust blows up to the size of a nickel and chases around the screen like a dust storm." Every bit of air that enters Nick's building gets scrubbed in water, oil, and electric filters. And the whole interior is kept under higher air pressure than the outside, so that when visitors come in from the dusty outdoors the vestibule out-draft brushes them off.

Later on, Nick would make the release prints of *Next Voice* for theatre exhibition; about 400 of them, most likely, and worth about $180 each (Technicolor prints of the same length would run around $600).

However, the story is trying to get ahead of itself.

Counting chickens before they're hatched isn't nearly as risky as making 400 release prints of a picture before your director has finished shooting it. While we have been exploring the back lot, Wellman has been shooting film at an unprecedented rate, and when you hear the rustle of the turning page the time will be exactly day fourteen.

18

Wednesday, March 8th. Everybody was running in overdrive. If we got the breaks, this could be the last day of shooting. Fourteen days; it just didn't seem possible. And, of course, maybe it wasn't.

As is usually the case with the final day or two of a schedule the crew wore their roller skates, moving all over the lot to pick up the bit shots and afterthoughts and tie-overs and tough ones you're so apt to push aside until the last minute. But the Lot 2 shot of the dog chasing newsboy Joe, estimated for half a day, went in on Take 1 in fifty minutes. The company moved back to the house set on 18 for montage bits, which were checked off shortly after lunch.

The early afternoon went to picking up a half dozen added angles on earlier scenes. I had worked with the cutters day by day, of course, screening each batch of footage and advising on its assembling, so that I had some feeling of the whole. Daily, I had passed along my reactions on various items to Wellman, and despite the rapid shooting he had already picked up most of the second thoughts; the occasional closeups I felt we needed, and the infrequent bits of business which might seem slightly overdrawn. This afternoon's work would about clean up that phase. I stayed up in my office out of Wellman's hair as long as I could stand it, but about four I came down to the set. I watched for a few minutes, and when Billy finished a setup I asked him if I could talk to the people for a minute.

I hadn't intended to say very much. They were all keyed high, rolling so fast and hot that I doubt if they'd have held still for much. And as it turned out, I said almost nothing. I got started all right, saying something I meant very sincerely about a great crew and a great cast and a great director. But then I made the mistake of looking into those wonderful faces, and pride and affection welled up in my throat and I finished up fast and got out of there before I made a star-spangled spectacle of myself. They went back to work, and after an hour of moving-automobile shots on the process stage, the company broke for supper.

While the crews loaded their trucks for the move-over to Lot 2, the staff walked to the cutters' projection room for the nightly ritual of screening the dailies. Sometimes called "rushes," the dailies are the previous day's takes on which Wellman had ordered, "Print it."

Camera, Sound, Wardrobe; each key man of the crew checks his own phase of the work, looking for the faults rather than the good points, but hoping that nothing will have to be retaken. These men absorb this confusing assortment of film in their stride, despite the fact that everything is out of context and the same action appears over and over from different angles, with the director or a grip walking off the scene at the beginning, the man with the chalk-numbered slate walking in, and the miscellaneous voices poking into the sound track here and there. (The cutters can snip any unwanted sounds out of the film so long as they do not overlap wanted sounds.) The spontaneous actions and lines of actors when they fluff sometimes become collector's items. Tonight's batch of footage is all fine, no problems. Somebody says, "Okay, we can come to work tomorrow," and the men head for supper.

Twilight has faded and the lights are on in the studio street when the staff ambles out of the commissary toward the waiting cars. The extras are coming in through the main gate and walking up the street toward the buses. "Forty men, thirty-five women, mixed ages, dignified types," per the teletype to Central Casting, "nice clothes, hats and coats, as would wear to church."

Over on Lot 2 the white colonial church stands immobile in the lights like a tranquil Gulliver as the busy Lilliputians swarm over and around him. The windows and the wide doors are already bright with incandescent yellow, and more lights are going in behind the fluted columns to give depth to the portico. Across the pleasant suburban street, a battery of huge sun arcs on spidery wooden towers bathes the street with blue-white light, casting the opaque shadows of night as they stand in for the moon. The night is cool, but not chilly, and there is little need for the red-glowing charcoal braziers which are spotted about. The coffee wagon is due any minute.

Wellman and Mellor are standing back on a lawn across the street, squinting at the layout as Joel barks orders through the electric megaphone to jam the street in front of the church with automobiles packed in four abreast. This is the seventh night of the play, that last night on which everybody in the world has crowded into the church of his choice. We want a preliminary shot of the packed street and the church portico crowded with people who cannot get in, and then the scene where two ushers force a passage through the crowd as Joe helps Mary out of the church and down the steps to start the trip to the hospital.

The last bus-load of extras rolls in, and Bill takes over the electric megaphone as he peers through the camera-finder and works out the composition of his shot. It works up quickly. In everybody there is that strange spirit of camaraderie which seems to infect the most blasé veteran on an outdoor night location—which they express by complaining about the cold, squawking about delayed coffee and otherwise beefing happily to cover up their unsophisticated feeling of excitement and adventure. Perhaps it's atavistic, going back to cavemen around a fire, but there is something mystic about that bright, up-welling pool of blue-white light in the all-encompassing black which seems to set these people off in a world populated only by themselves for these few hours.

Both of the long shots went in on Take 1, and the crew moved in for the close stuff. And there, on what could be the windup of the picture, came a hitch.

To an outsider, it would have looked fine: the two ushers pushed a passage through the crowd, Mary and Joe came into camera and moved off toward their car. Candidly, I think I would have bought it myself. But Bill didn't like it. He couldn't put his finger for the moment on exactly what was the matter, just insisted, "It doesn't ring right." He ran it through again. This time he spotted the trouble.

He took the actors aside and told them that they had to force their way through the crowd a lot faster. Then he sent the cast off for coffee and told the extras confidentially that the actors were coming through much too fast, so jam in together more tightly on the porch and shove them back. It worked fine. Between Jim and Nancy trying to make Bill happy by lunging through the crowd faster, and the crowd trying to make Bill even happier by preventing the stars from moving at all, the look of pure desperation on those two faces is strictly authentic.

Bill dismissed the extras and took the crew over on the New York street to pick up the last two flashes of the montage where Joe is searching the streets for young Johnny.

Nancy stayed behind in her trailer dressing-room, and after she had changed her clothes she just sat there for a while. All of a sudden she was realizing that it was over, that she wouldn't be coming to the studio tomorrow to be Mary Smith. It seemed as though she'd been Mary Smith as long as she could remember, and she'd sort of taken it for granted that she would always keep on being Mary Smith, and now it was over. It was a very empty feeling, and the girl whom this picture was going to make into a great star sat by herself in a trailer dressing-room feeling lonely and forlorn.

Then a prop man poked his head in the trailer door and said, "Can I have your wedding ring and prayer book?" He added, "Mr. Wellman was looking for you. We want you at the party." And Nancy felt fine. This was the wonderful thing about pictures. The theatre was wonderful, too, but out here you *belonged* somewhere. People called you "we."

Over under a lamp post on the New York street Joe walked up to a newsboy, asked him a question; the newsboy shook his head, Wellman said, "That's the *one*," Bill Hole wrote "CLOSED PRODUCTION" across scene 114x3A, and some wit topped the old move-over cliché with, "We're on the wrong lot." First thing in the morning, a very grateful producer would start a jeweler engraving St. Genesius medals for each of the members of a great company.

Another director might have had a very posh party at a
night spot. Not Bill: this party was pure Wellman, a very
nice array of food and drinks set out under a battery of
work lights on a Lot 2 street corner. There was that wonderful healthy-tired feeling which comes after a stretch
run, and the warm friendliness of people who have proved
themselves to each other. Soon they'd break up; tomorrow
or next week they'd be pushing other pictures with other
people, but tonight they were a unit. Somebody had given
Nancy some champagne and she broke it out, and after a
little while the fellows began coming up to shake hands
with Wellman and check out for home. There was a little
stammer in everybody's voice, everybody's heart was beating a little faster. No matter how many you've done, it's
always a thrill to put another one away. And tomorrow,
everybody would get a haircut.

PART FOUR

Finishing the Picture

19

Making a picture is, in one small way, like fighting a battle. The exciting and adventurous part of the job which catches the public's interest is quickly over. But it was preceded by a long period of preparation, and must be followed by an arduous and unglamorous mopping-up operation.

When Bill Hole wrote CLOSED PRODUCTION across his script, the picture was far from finished. To switch analogies, it was in the stage of a garment for which the cloth has been cut to pattern and laid out on the tailor's bench. There still were several essential operations to be done on *Next Voice* in the way of assembling and fitting and trimming. To say nothing of putting it in the show window and catching the interest of the customers.

These several finishing operations would be done by small specialized teams, working simultaneously in different parts of the lot. The editors would have to cut the picture together for the showing of the first rough-cut, and keep on improving it until at last the negative was cut and the picture frozen. Somebody would have to shoot the numerous insert scenes of newspapers, watch faces, feet, and what not. There might be some montage work to be done, and certainly the lab must supply the numerous dissolves and fades and other optical effects. Certain bits of dialogue which had been obscured in recording by extraneous sounds would have to be "looped" on the dialogue stage by the actors. The multitude of sound effects must be inserted or added, the title and background music must be composed and recorded. Then all of these would have to be combined in the re-recording rooms before we could take the picture out for its sneak preview, see what more work was needed, and at last wind up the studio operation with the okayed answer print.

The moment the camera stops turning, everything becomes double rush. Nevertheless this finishing phase invariably uses much more time than was consumed in the actual shooting; the average picture consumes two or three months or more, even without retakes. And most of it is work of a highly creative order which has a tremendous influence on the entertainment value of the picture as it finally flashes on the theatre screen.

This finishing phase of *Next Voice* took six weeks.

20

Day by day during the shooting, the exposed film of both pictures and sound had been delivered to the studio lab, developed overnight, and fed into the routine in the form of positive prints.

Each day's batch of *Next Voice* prints, together with the "dailies" of all other productions in work on the lot, filtered down through a series of private projection rooms. Sound's Doug Shearer, Camera's John Arnold, Lab's Nickolaus, Art's Gibbons, Supervising Film Editor Margaret Booth and others checked every foot for possible flaws in their various specialties, alert to correct any dangerous trends which might seem to be creeping in, with particular care to ensure that nothing unfortunate was happening to the stars. In the Continuity Room, Gloria Colone and her girls clicked the footage through their moviolas and typed the description of the action and dialogue in each take, one sheet to each, which would accumulate day by day to a sort of as-shot script. The *Next Voice* footage usually got over to my projection room in the late afternoon, and after I had put in my session with Jack Dunning, the editor on the picture, he took it over to his cutting room.

Perhaps in the next year or so when the industry shifts over entirely to safety-base film the cutters can work in more comfortable surroundings, but now everything is fireproof except the film and the people. The two-story concrete building is a geometrical collection of concrete hallways and concrete cubicles, the dominant decoration being overhead piping, sprinkler heads, and metal-clad doors. The prevailing smell is acetone and carbon tet, and the prevailing sound is a weird concatenation of screeches and squawks and beautiful voices and uproars from a dozen busy moviolas.

The walls of Jack Dunning's cubicle are lined with racks of shiny square cans which contain the sorted and indexed takes of *Next Voice*. His moviola, an instrument which looks like a man-sized insect of all legs, arms and reels, with one glaring glass eye, is a sort of personal movie machine on which he can run his strips of sound and picture film in synchronization. The sound from the primitive little speaker is rather squawky, and he views the picture as it passes under a three-inch magnifying lens, but he can move the film through at any speed, forward or reverse, stop it anywhere, and make any necessary marks on it with a colored grease pencil. The film in work spills into a big white canvas basket. The strips of cut takes awaiting disposition hang down from serried hooks into a similar container, and the standard furniture of the metal bench is a shiny precision sprocket-wheeled synchronizer and the rumbling rewind. The cutter's identifying badge is a loose white cotton glove on his left hand. His other occupational tag is a tanned face, because he has to go out of the building and stand in the sun whenever he wants to smoke.

In the early days of motion pictures there were no cutters; the function of editing didn't even exist. The cameraman-director of the turn of the century took it for granted that he had to shoot his scenes in their exact dramatic continuity. He removed the exposed rolls of film from his camera, developed and printed them, and that—unchanged—

was the movie which went on the screen. But then an unsung genius named Edwin S. Porter demonstrated the simple but revolutionary idea that the roll of film was not sacred from the touch of human hands, that by the use of scissors and cement he could reassort the continuity of the scenes on the original roll. And it was Porter's epic picture *The Great Train Robbery* (its real contribution was overshadowed by its distinction as the first "feature") which proved on a practical scale that this new "assembled" film medium could go beyond mere peep-show incidents and tell a full, rounded, dramatic story.

Perhaps this doesn't sound very important. But on your mental screen please flash a big face closeup of Joe Smith, his eyes looking upward. Now follow it with a picture of a street sign. Obviously Joe, in his closeup, was searching for an address. Now cancel that out, and imagine Joe's closeup is followed instead by a picture of a bunch of bananas. We were wrong in our first guess about the closeup; obviously Joe was hungry. But suppose Joe's closeup is followed by the picture of an airplane taking off—or a dead boy at Joe's feet on the sidewalk—or any of a hundred other varied images. See what happens? The meaning of any one little strip of film can be *changed*, according to the picture which precedes it and the picture which follows it. The editor knows this as he assorts and reassorts the continuity of his scenes, and the angles within his scenes, and he uses this power not only to keep the audience clearly informed of what is going on, but so to arrange his accents that he increases his dramatic and entertainment values. He is really a sort of director.

Many scenes give the cutter no particular problem. The bits, the tie-overs, the minor scenes which merely carry along the narrative with no particular emotion usually reach the cutter in a form of a single take. His only job here is usually to trim off a slow start or an anti-climactic finish.

Incidentally, audiences have become so conditioned to the film medium that we can move a picture much faster nowadays. You'll notice that in today's pictures actors don't make a definite entrance into a scene, transact their dramatic business, and then say good-bye and walk out (except when the actual arrival or departure makes some dramatic point). We cut instantaneously from the meat of one scene to the meat of another, coming in on each scene as close as we can get to its high point and still remain intelligible, and cutting away to the next scene the instant that the point has been made. Sometimes we cut even before a minor point has actually been nailed down, the editor cutting away as soon as it becomes obvious to the audience what would happen if we kept on hanging around.

There's a good little example of this trimming technique in the *Next Voice* script, at the beginning of Scene 23. It's on the first evening: Joe has just told Mary and Johnny about hearing the Voice and he has walked out of the bedroom trying to figure out who was trying to sound like God on the radio. Young Johnny has suggested it might be a young radio ham up the street. Scene 23, in the hallway outside the bedroom, originally read:

> *Joe rubs his neck, thinks hard. He shakes his head, walks to the phone, dials a number.*
> JOE (*into phone*)
> Gus? Joe . . . Say, was your kid fooling with the radio just now . . . ?

The instruction to Joe probably served its purpose in telling Jim Whitmore what his attitude should be. But when you see this sequence on the screen it will cut directly from Mary in the bedroom to Joe just starting to talk into the telephone.

Sometimes the cutter will make radical changes in the order of the scenes. Sometimes whole scenes and even sequences will be thrown into that white canvas basket which serves as the traditional cutting-room floor. Sometimes individual scenes will be so reassorted internally that their whole emphasis and consequence is turned upside down. But when a good script has been well directed and shot, most of the editor's work is on the shot-by-shot progression inside the value scenes.

Nevertheless, he still has many vital decisions to make. On *Next Voice* 55,000 feet of "print it" takes came into that concrete cell, and the finished film went out at a length of 7,630 feet. The difference represents the decisions.

Jack Dunning had studied the script until he knew it thoroughly. He dropped over to the set once or twice every day during the shooting to see what was in Wellman's mind, and he and Margaret Booth and I would talk over the layout of the scenes when we ran the dailies in my projection room. By the time the dailies came over to his cubicle and assistant cutter Greydon Gilmer had cut up and indexed the rolls, the scenes had usually shaken themselves down in Jack's mind into a rough plan and progression.

Much of Jack's work went to keep his function from being recognized. Any cut which the audience notices is a bad cut. Good cutting looks like no cutting; the editor

cuts from one shot to another on something that distracts
the audience's attention for an instant, such as a gesture, a
look, a sound, the opening of a door or anything that makes
the cut quicker than the eye. Your blink, by the way, lasts
five frames, while the cut takes only one.

I once heard a learned lecturer state that a primary purpose of cutting in films was to provide visual variety. "The
eye tires of any fixed viewpoint after a very few seconds,"
he said, "and must be refreshed by a change of angle."
Actually, any scene which can go dull without changes of
angle was a dull scene to begin with, for visual variety is a
by-product of editing rather than a reason for it.

The editor assorts his cuts to place accent and emphasis,
to build laughs and keep them spinning, to justify the tears,
to flesh out the characters with significant touches, to put
over plot points, to establish plants subtly in the audience's
mind, to demonstrate relationships and connect up cause
and effect, to build importance and give emphasis, to build
suspense—to do all this by guiding the audience's curiosity
at certain times and following its curiosity at others—to
project the changing moods of the story in terms of pace
and tempo and, above all, to keep the human line of the
story strong and clear and alive in terms of the characters'
emotional reactions.

All this perhaps sounds very abstract. I'll grant that I
have never known a cutter to analyze very deeply the reasons why he prefers one cut over another. He just feels it
that way; years of working with film has given him a subconscious feeling for tempo and pace. He is, however, always conscious of the need to show the emotional reaction
of his characters. He knows that a movie in its essence is
simply a progression of reactions. An action itself, to the

audience, is only a sort of trigger, which immediately sets off the question, "How does so-and-so *feel* about this?"

Imagine a newsreel shot of a Chinese village which has just been bombed. A young woman is lying on the street, her body mangled like the others. The newsreel camera-man's lens may go in close enough for you to see the grue-some details, but your emotions aren't really stirred beyond the tsk-tsk stage. But now the camera pans. A little way down the street a mite of a child in a kimono is picking her way among the bodies. She's looking for someone, peering at the faces. Suddenly it hits you—did the cameraman show you that young woman on purpose, was it a plant? The child walks up the street, and your stomach muscles tighten; she comes closer to the dead young woman, closer, closer. . . . The child sees her, stares for one awful moment—then throws herself down on the dead woman's breast and sobs. You, the audience, are torn apart by the sight. But what tore you apart was not the tragedy of the death, not the action—it was the emotional result, *the reaction of a character in whom you had taken an interest.*

Coming back to story films, you may have noticed that as soon as a given speech has gone far enough so that the audience can guess out the rest of it, the picture cuts from the speaker to the hearer as the speech continues off-scene. Reason: to catch the reaction, to see what emotional effect that speech is going to have on the character to whom it's addressed. The term "action pictures" is often applied to low-budget western and other fast-moving films of the sort which usually appear on the lower half of double bills. There is significance in the fact that the pictures which command and sway the great audiences could well be called "reaction pictures."

All of this most certainly calls for a concrete example out of *Next Voice*. A little earlier we saw how Wellman shot the pickups of added angles and reaction closeups for Scene 22. This was the scene on the first evening where Joe came into young Johnny's bedroom to tell about the strange voice on the radio which claimed to be God. The master shot of the over-all scene (the full shot looking across Johnny and Mary toward Joe in the doorway) told the story adequately, but it would not "milk" the scene of its shock, suspense and emotional values. Wellman knew this. That's why he shot the pickups.

Dunning's first decision was to "play it on the boy," to insert closeups of young Johnny which would indicate his feeling that "Pop is unusually worked up, what's wrong?" And he wanted to spin the scene out, hold it back with suspense and set an entrance for Joe's important disclosure, the keystone of the whole story. He would do this not by adding footage, for he was committed to the time-span of the dialogue as recorded, but he could slow down the scene in its apparent tempo by cutting from closeup to closeup on the individual lines. So here is that scene in a sort of cutting continuity, showing how the shots were chosen and assorted, with an over-simplified indication of Jack's reasoning on each cut.

Which shot?	INT. JOHNNY'S ROOM—NIGHT

Cutter thinks: "We'll establish the place and the people."

22D (12 Sec)	MARY AND JOHNNY *medium 2-shot*	*Mary is sewing as young Johnny, at desk, in pajamas, struggles over his homework.* JOHNNY (*mumbling*)· Bring down the nine . . . another nine . . . *The off-scene radio shuts off. Mary looks up, toward door.*

Audience wants to know: "Who's there?"

22A (17 Sec)	*Full shot over* MARY *and* JOHNNY *across whole room toward doorway*	*The door opens,* JOE *steps a little way in. He seems puzzled.* MARY· What is it, Joe? *Joe just shakes his head.* MARY. Finish the dishes? JOE. Huh? Oh, sure . . . yeah . . . MARY You're not listening to the radio. What's wrong? JOE: Kind of a funny thing—on the radio just now—they announced it was exactly eight-thirty— JOHNNY (*mocking*) Garry Gavery, the Golden Voiced Goon— MARY: Quiet, Johnny. JOE (*oddly puzzled*): Yeah, they announced it . . . (*cut to*)

Audience: "What's he acting so oddly about?"

22B (9 Sec)	JOE, *waist closeup* (*in doorway*)	JOE (*continuing*): . . . then there was kind of an odd empty sound. Then a voice said, "This is God. I will be with you for the next few days. . . ."

Which shot?		Cutter: "Let's show 'em how important this is."

Cutter: "Let's show 'em how important this is."

| 22F (1 Sec) | JOHNNY, *waist c.u.* | *The boy looks up, startled.* (*Silence*) |

Audience: "Does Mary agree it's so important?"

| 22E (2 Sec) | MARY, *waist c u.* | MARY (*taken aback*): What? |

Audience: "Does Joe really believe this stuff?"

| 22C (6 Sec) | JOE, *face closeup* | JOE (*puzzled*): A Voice said, "This is God. I will be with you for the next few days." |

Cutter: "Let's build the reactions a little higher."

| 22D (4 Sec) | MARY *and* JOHNNY *medium 2-shot* | MARY Then what happened? |

Audience: "Yeah, what did happen, Joe?"

| 22B (8 Sec) | JOE, *waist c.u.* | JOE: Nothing happened—the program came back on. . . . MARY: Maybe it was just the introduction. . . . JOE No—because when the program came back on Garry was in the middle of his first song . . . |

Cutter: "Let's keep the full scene alive."

| 22A (13 Sec) | *Full shot—whole room across* MARY *and* JOHNNY *toward* JOE *in door* | MARY (*thinking hard*). It must be one of those Mystery Voice shows. You have to guess whose voice . . JOE. But they never do that until after they tell you about the prizes. . . . MARY Or maybe it was one of those Orson Welles things. . . . |

Which
shot?

JOHNNY. I got it! It was young Eddie Boyle. He's always trying to be a radio ham. Maybe he cut in.

Cutter: "Let's set Joe up for the boy's big line."

22B
(5 Sec)

JOE, *waist c u.*

JOE· Well, if that isn't the silliest . . . Would Eddie Boyle's voice sound like God?

Audience: "What about it, son?"

22F
(3 Sec)

JOHNNY, *waist c.u.*

JOHNNY: I don't know. I never heard God.

Cutter: "That calls for something
from his mother."

22E
(2 Sec)

MARY, *waist c.u.*

MARY. That's not very nice, Johnny. Go to bed.

Cutter: "Let's finish on the over-all relationship."

22A
(8 Sec)

*Full shot—whole room
across* MARY *and*
JOHNNY *toward*
JOE *at door*

JOE· Yeah . . .

(Joe exits through door.)

MARY: Go ahead, Johnny, get into bed.

(Scene
Length:
90 Sec)

(She kisses Johnny, turns, follows Joe out and closes the door.)

Next scene: "What are Joe and Mary
going to do about this?"

Day by day during the shooting, Dunning had cut together his takes into rough assemblies. The picture had been shot so fast as to make it practically impossible for a cutter to keep up. But I found a way to make all of this previous rush look like paradise. I couldn't help it; an opportunity arose that was just too good to miss.

Visiting the studio from their New York headquarters
were William F. Rodgers, in charge of sales for the company, and Howard Dietz, in charge of all Loew's exploitation and advertising. The success of the picture with the
public would depend very considerably on the push which
these two men and their departments put behind it. I
wanted them to see the picture while I was present so that
I could answer their objections, take advantage of good
ideas that they might have for changes, and perhaps instill
in them some of my own enthusiasm. We finished principal
photography, as you will remember, on a Wednesday night.
Mr. Dietz was leaving the coast Friday afternoon.

Anybody would admit that it was impossible to put even
a clumsy rough-cut on the screen in a few short hours. But
at ten A.M. Friday morning the film went on the screen in
a downstairs projection room of the Administration Building. And it was not clumsy. It had none of the fades nor
dissolves nor opticals which smooth the flow of a finished
film. It lacked vital sound effects and had no music, and the
dramatic highpoints frequently fizzled out in a title-card
SCENE MISSING, but it was a well-organized job of telling a
straightforward emotional story. In addition to the two
New York men, Benny Thau was there to see how Whitmore and·Davis had handled their first assignments as stars,
and Howard Strickling and Frank Whitbeck had brought
their studio exploitation and advertising people. I sat
through the showing with my stomach flipping over and
over as nervously as though I were trying to get my first
job in the business. And if Wellman was as calm as he claims
why did he chew his pipe in two?

The lights went up into a dead silence. I stood it as long
as I could. Then I essayed a nervous laugh and said, "Is

everybody dead?" It turned out that they liked it. They liked it well enough to throw all their very considerable weight behind getting it to the public. Even Wellman was pleased. But the greatest compliment seemed to me to be the reddened eyes of Jack Dunning and Gil, because when your picture gets to the emotions of its cutters, you've really got something. So I said to the boys, "You've run this picture so many times, I think it's wonderful it can make you cry."

"Who's crying?" said Dunning, rubbing his eyes, "we were squinting into moviolas until three o'clock this morning."

Jack and Gil took the film back to their cubicle. We'd make minor alterations, smooth out the flow during the next few weeks, but there would be no extensive retakes nor major changes.

And, more importantly at the moment, the film was close enough to final version to start the several remaining specialized teams on their contributions.

21

Back in the really plush days it was not uncommon for a director to expect his initial shooting schedule to produce only a sort of first draft. With this in hand he could see where the story sagged, what the problems were, and then he would go ahead and really make the picture in the retakes. Said retakes might run into weeks of time and hundreds of thousands of dollars. Nowadays we prefer to find and solve our problems before the overhead starts, and *Next Voice* was a fortunate and rather typical example of the new practice.

Nevertheless, on any quality picture which expects to play the top first-run houses, a certain amount of post-production patching and trimming is expected. We allow for it on both picture and sound.

Most of our second thoughts on *Next Voice* were shot on that final Wednesday of the schedule, without added cost. There were six shots, all in the house or garage and all rather routine. They ranged from a new angle on young Johnny coming in for breakfast on the first morning, to give him a more sympathetic entrance, to a new shot of Aunt Ethel in the armchair after the false-labor scene, which would give that strong scene a stronger curtain.

Our closest approach to retakes was one morning about a week after close of production. Joe and Mary and Aunt Ethel came to Stage 18 to re-do two short bits which played so well in the rough cut that I thought a slightly different treatment would build them into high points. The crew started setting up their equipment at ten o'clock, and by ten-thirty-seven Mellor had lighted and Wellman had rehearsed and shot three takes on the beginning of Scene 78, Aunt Ethel's initial entrance. Then we swung over to the scene where Joe wakes up at home after the saloon sequence. Wellman and the two actors viewed the film of the previously-shot scene on a moviola which had been brought over to the stage, refreshing their memories sufficiently to make the new action match exactly with the footage into which it would be cut. At eleven-twenty Wellman had what he wanted, the actors checked out and the crew stayed around to shoot a screen test of a new girl the studio was considering. Our retake expense ran ten minutes short of an hour and a half.

Of course, some post-production photography is routine and already allowed for in the budget. On *Next Voice*, this work consisted mostly of inserts. These are the closeup shots of newspapers, clocks and other props, without action other than perhaps a slight movement of a hand. If an insert shot does show action, it is of a very close-up and detailed character, such as a finger pulling a trigger. Inserts almost never require the presence of the original actor, which is why many of them are held over until the finish of production. The closeup inserts of Joe's foot pressing the starter pedal of his car required definite character acting to project the irritation, fear and surprise which Joe felt on the different occasions. Those we had picked up during the schedule.

Most of our inserts were shot on Stage 18 the day after the close of production. Many people even within the industry have an impression that inserts are shot with special equipment in special quarters, but that is seldom the case unless the insert presents some special problem, such as panning around a map, or showing germs under a microscope.

There were seven extras on the call, most of them people whom we had seen recognizably in the church as they looked down at their watches. Now we'd photograph the closeup faces of the watches themselves, coming progressively closer to the fateful eight-thirty and the anticipated Voice of God.

The camera setup on inserts is usually very simple. This was a silent camera, looking bony and naked without its protective blimp. The lighting setup was also simple; one broad with silks, one Junior with a gobo shade to shape its beam, and a couple of midgets. The camera lens came down within inches of the watch faces and there was trouble with the reflections of the light in the crystals until somebody got the revolutionary idea of taking the crystals out.

Next, stand-in Jack Harris slipped the newspaper bag over his head, stood on a grass mat, and held the newspaper in his hand while the camera read the "God Speaks on Radio" headline over his shoulder. Then the church radio set which we see in closeup on the pulpit in that tense moment of silence was brought over from the Stage 19 church and photographed on the counter of the montage drug store.

The last insert was of the poster in the hospital waiting room on which the Stork is saying, "I've never lost a father yet." That also was on 19 but we brought it over to the setup, hung the hospital clock above the poster, and prepared to shoot. Somebody called attention to the second hand on the electric clock; people would notice that it didn't move during the three or four seconds of the shot.

But electric clocks run only on alternating current, and so the closing shot of the picture featured gaffer Philbrick patching together a hundred feet of cord and searching the clutter of the stage walls for the AC outlet. When and if you see the picture, the studio will appreciate your glancing up from the stork and admiring the beautiful way in which that second hand goes round and round.

When a sound mixer is having trouble trying to record dialogue against the interference of other sounds, the jargon has it that he's "fighting 2A."

Stage 2A, just across the alley from the Sound Department, is the place where dialogue voices and sound effects are recorded for sound only, without camera, by synchronizing supervisor Ted Hoffman.

Some of the dialogue work on 2A is repair work; some of it you might call new construction. In the latter category would fall the session following close of production when we recorded radio commentators Cecil Brown, Chet Huntley, Lou Merrill and others in the speeches which would come out of the assorted radios to report what the Voice had said and how the world was taking it. 2A is much like a radio studio, with Hoffman working in a monitor's booth behind a soundproof glass window, and these readings were the daily bread and butter of the professional announcers we had cast. I wanted to experiment a little with the degree of excitement to be given the various speeches, and so on, but the takes clicked in with no particular problem.

Ordinarily we would have recorded these segments prior to production and played them back on the set as the scenes were shot. But there had not been sufficient time, and so

now Jack Dunning held the stop-watch to make sure each
speech would fit in the hole which the actors had left for it.

Connie Kahn had fought the good fight and, in spite of
the rapid production, there was very little repair work to
do on the dialogue itself. Some of the work resulted from
changes. We had to switch the name of the radio station
from the KIH of the script to the KWTA which the FCC
cleared for us, so all dialogue containing the outlawed letters had to be newly recorded. Joe's remark at the second breakfast about not needing Mr. Brannan's three cents,
when viewed in the light of today's newspaper prices, gave
us the air of a period picture, so the line was newly recorded with a price of seven cents.

But most of the repairs were concerned with dialogue
lines where words were indistinct or blotted out by extraneous noises. For example, Joe had made part of his speech
of reconciliation with Aunt Ethel while walking on his
crumpled newspaper. Again, in the scene in Brannan's
workshop where Joe squares himself with his young son,
certain essential words had been scratched by the noise of
Johnny's sandpapering. Most of this repeat recording was
done by a very interesting process known as "looping."
—.Take Joe's line, "Even if you're sore at me, Johnny—
don't forget, it's Mom who takes the beating." All the way
through this line on the screen, young Johnny was showing
his emotion by sandpapering like mad and the excess sandpapering had to be wiped out from under the dialogue.

The stage was darkened. The strip of film containing
the original faulty line had been cut out and cemented into
a loop, and the sound was fed to the actor over and over
through earphones until he had soaked in its mood and

tempo. Then the sound was fed him as the picture was projected on the screen and he watched his mouth movement
on the syllables. Joe practiced until he could exactly duplicate what he was hearing, in perfect "lip sync," then signaled that he was ready and watched his lips in the picture
as he spoke the new line into the mike.

This process can be extraordinarily useful. Sometimes,
especially in very noisy action pictures, and films which
are shot largely on location, almost the entire dialogue may
be looped. In an emergency we can operate on an actor
whose voice is wrong in some way to give him a completely new voice. With luck we can even change a few
actual words, usually for legal reasons. All this can be particularly useful now that Hollywood is making many pictures abroad, with foreign actors.

This phase of the work is exacting, of course, but it's
mechanical. The creative side of 2A begins to fizz when
Mike Steinore's boys check in to make some of the sound
effects.

For example, Joe's line of dialogue above had been sliced
away from the sandpapering, and now the sandpapering
would have to be put back in the track to match the pic-
tured action exactly, though in such a way that it would
no longer interfere with the dialogue. That, among many
other things, would be Mike Steinore's responsibility.

On March 17th Mike and his brood got their duplicate
print of *Next Voice*. Over in one of the projection rooms
in the cutters' alley, they ran the reels and laid out the job.
"Kenny and Finn take Reel 4," said Steinore, and Finn went
over under a hooded light to watch the picture and mark

the needed effects on his pad, checking the illuminated footage counter at the bottom of the screen to catch the point at which each effect must start and stop.

Many sounds will be left just as they were recorded on set along with the dialogue. Others will be "sweetened," the actual effect reinforced to achieve the added prominence or significance which Mike feels needed. Other effects will be supplied from scratch. "Lay in some new footsteps along here, less woody". . . . "Put in a good door-close". . . . "Let's feed in some light traffic behind this exterior."

Sound effects can add a whole new dimension to a picture, and vastly increase its scope. The sound of automobiles and the clanging of trolley-car bells supply the traffic outside the cocktail bar which was lacking when we shot the scene inside Stage 18. And when Joe is walking the dark street in search of his son the distant whistle of a train underscores his mood. Because of the desirability of recording clear dialogue, practically all the sounds you hear in A-budget pictures were added to the film long after the actual scenes were shot, and this includes all kinds of sounds, from the obvious footsteps and doorbells and automobile pull-aways to purely atmospheric backgrounds of crickets at night and the buzzing of flies on a sylvan Sunday afternoon.

The thousands of little rolls of stock film indexed in Mike's library vault contain almost every imaginable noise and nuance thereof. Mixer Kahn had co-operated by recording wild takes of atmospheric sounds on the various *Next Voice* locations, particularly the hard-to-duplicate specialized sounds in the aircraft factory. And the boys had recorded an assortment of special sounds on Joe's beat-up old car one afternoon on a street in the back lot.

As Mike's boys ran each picture reel across their benches, they "built" the two or three or four auxiliary tracks of sound effects which that reel would need. The effects, on their short strips of sound film, were carefully laid into reel-long lengths of blank film until each effect was so placed that it would speak up in exact synchronization with the action of the picture. When several effects would have to occur in a cluster, they were spread around on different tracks so each could be separately controlled and balanced in. Later, the whole collection of sound tracks would be combined with dialogue and music onto the one master track which would be printed on the theatre version.

Most of the effects in any movie come from the stock library. Mike's boys can choose, for example, between 284 different dog barks, and every mixer who returns from a location turns in a few more effects which he has recorded on helpful speculation. But in every picture some of the effects must be specially recorded. Footsteps, for example, are so individual in spirit that stock sound never seems exactly right. And so, sooner or later, the deal ends up back with Ted Hoffman on 2A.

You don't notice it until the boys begin making their peculiar noises, but the floor of 2A looks like the display of a mad flooring contractor with its patchwork squares of concrete, brick, hardwood blocks, rubber tile, felt, carpet, and flagstone. Plus some large wooden pans where one may walk on dirt or gravel or through weeds or water or mud. The soundproofed stage is properly dead, but Ted

can get the bouncy effect of auditoriums or outdoors by
routing the sound through a concrete room called an echo
chamber, adding whatever he wants in the way of rain-
barrel reverberation to the original sound.

It was late in March when Scott Perry and Harold Hum-
brock recorded three special sound sequences for *Next
Voice* on which stock effects would not serve. The first
one was from the first evening of the picture, when Joe
comes into the living room from the kitchen with a glass in
his hand, picks up the newspaper, walks over to the leather
easy chair, sits down, and opens the paper. Scott donned
acoustically matching heavy shoes and hard-fabric trousers
from the supply lockers, Harold placed a strip of carpet
over the linoleum floor at the proper breaking point a few
feet from the leather chair, and prepared to handle the
clink of the glass. As the projectionist darkened the stage
and ran the strip of picture while the boys rehearsed it for
synchronization, I suddenly realized how complex a perfectly ordinary sequence of human movement can be. Ted
was satisfied on Take 3; the glass clink was a little high but,
"We can paint it down on the track."

Joe had delivered his son's newspapers on the outdoor
location, where we could not possibly have gotten micro-
phones in position to record his movements. Yet the audience would expect to hear on the screen his feet hitting the
concrete and the newspaper plopping into the bushes. So
Scott walked in the changing rhythms of Joe on the screen,
from concrete to brick to grass; and after some experi-
menting to satisfy Ted, Harold threw the paper so that it
would land in the bush with a glancing impact rather than
a flat drop. Everybody adds "little touches" to the film as
he does his part of the work, and it's a summary of all the

touches which makes realism: here, Ted noted that Joe let his left foot drag momentarily on his final step, as most of us do, instead of coming to a military halt. The last job of the afternoon, that of completing the illusion of Mr. Brannan watering his lawn, was performed by the forthright device of having Harold squirt a hose on a pan of earth, adjusting the nozzle as Ted listened to the sound over the loudspeaker and spoke his directions over the talk-back. "Fine it up a little; get a hiss. . . . No, now it sounds like frying. . . . Don't keep squirting it in the same place, it's getting muddy and loud."

In every picture there is some one spot where the impact stands or falls on the success of a sound effect. In *Next Voice*, it was the rain on the third evening. The radio announcer reported God as having said, "Are you afraid because you believe that you have earned another forty days and forty nights of rain? Must I perform such miracles in order to make you believe?" On the screen Joe switched off the radio, and he and Mary and Johnny stayed silent and unmoving as the words sank in. Then must come the sound of rain which, building rapidly until it seemed to be fulfilling the prophecy, would throw our characters together in a climax of mortal fear in the face of God's wrath.

This problem would have been a challenge under any circumstances, but here it was made almost impossible by the fact that we could not show the visible rain in the picture. The sounds of many actions are amazingly alike, and human ears need the help of an image or some other clue to make identification. In radio broadcasting, for example, the dialogue will notify the audience whether the sound effect is an earthquake or an automobile crash or a collapsing chair, but the key sound of each effect may be the

crunching of the same old strawberry box. We had the
further complication that real rain covers such a wide frequency of sound waves that "effects rain" must be recreated, to fall within the limits of our electronic equipment.

Mike and the boys decided to build a little production
sequence on this. The sound begins with a few big drops
hitting a window pane. Then a very distant suggestion of
thunder. Then a scurry of drops across the pane in a crescendo which brings Joe to the window, then a crash of
near thunder and a deluge of rain and build it from there.

Wellman had directed the scene so that Joe becomes a
representative of all men in the face of the Eternal, trying
to protect their loved ones and knowing their failure. The
climax image on the screen has the quality of a statue. The
statue now rests on a solid base of sound.

22

There is comparatively little music in the *Next Voice;* in fact, there is startlingly little. But what is there is terribly important.

I have a great respect for the power of background music in dramatic film. Fundamental expressions of universal emotions sometimes drop below the level of a verbalization, and there the film can speak in the universal language of music. Music can heighten the significance and broaden the scope of great scenes, and may even add to a mediocre scene an importance which was lacking in the unscored version. We may depend on music to guide the audience's mood economically, using a single chord or short phrase to replace several feet of scene. We expect music to point up action, enrich emotions, bridge transitions, and particularly to weave the whole picture into unity with thematic threads of musical continuity.

Darryl Zanuck's deservedly successful film *Pinky* was laid out to carry a musical background under 125 of its 130 minutes of running time. The decision to take *Next Voice* to the public without the support of background scoring was not an easy one to make.

A good deal has been written about music in films, much of it with the unconscious assumption that the film exists as a background for the advancement of music. I have seen nothing written on the subject from the point of view of the producer, to whom music is one of several important

elements which he must blend and balance in terms of a
fused "whole."

In deciding the *Next Voice* problem I was guided by
some good advice which David Selznick had given me
many years ago. Selznick, who has employed music as successfully as any producer in films, told me never to be overcome by music and not to be afraid of it—to be tough
in my decisions, determining for myself when music was
needed and when it would be out of place, and to let no
one dissuade me once an honest decision had been reached.
I had the feeling that in this particular film, had I been
working with Selznick, he would have advised me to omit
all background scoring; that extensive scoring would impair
the whole style of the picture.

Nevertheless, the producer who is not a schooled mu-
sician should keep a coolly objective eye on his own
technical limitations. It was generally agreed that we would
use a hymn-like theme for the music which, by scoring the
main title and end title, would encourage a proper emotional approach to the picture in its beginning and solidify
the feeling which the audience would take away at the end.
One evening while I was running the picture at home a
melody floated into my mind. Next day I tried it out on
Johnny Green, head of the studio's Music Department. I
hummed it to him and he jotted the notes on paper, probably improving it as he went along. At first John viewed it
with some skepticism, thinking it had probably come more
from memory than inspiration, but a check disclosed that
it was really an original piece of music.

But David Raksin, the excellent young composer whom
Johnny had assigned to *Next Voice,* had already worked
out a hymn of his own. So both of the hymns were orches-

trated, and Johnny made rough recordings of them. I suppose I had a natural pride of authorship (a pride which always seems most marked when a fellow does something out of his normal field) and so it was a particularly difficult task for me to sit in one of the sound rooms as the two melodies were played back and make a decision between them.

The difficulty increased when I sensed that Raksin's hymn was a lot better than mine. But I was darned if I'd make the decision too quickly, so I turned to Wellman, who didn't know that the first selection was the one I had "composed," and asked him which he liked. He said, "My God, there's no question about it. The second one is wonderful and that first thing should be taken out and buried." I gulped and said we'd use the second one, and afterwards I told Wellman about the situation. He said, "Well, I'm very sorry, but even if I'd known I'd still have had to tell you to take it out and bury it."

It was March 17th before the work print was sufficiently complete to run it for the Music Department. Apart from the title music, we would need certain "justified" music, in the several situations where a radio set was playing in the scene. But we would take the picture to preview with "canned track" from our stock of library music, and later David would compose music which, though it must seem like ordinary radio fare, would blend with and enrich the emotional content of whatever human action was taking place on the screen. To Dave, that was pure routine. What about the considerable dramatic background scoring which would normally go into a picture of this sort?

After considerable discussion, with some strong convictions exhibited on both sides, I made the decision mentioned above. The script, the director, and the actors had achieved such extraordinary human realism that the introduction into any scene of a theatrical device, no matter how beautifully handled, might shatter the realism and thus destroy the very mood the music would be trying to build.

Film makes a terrifying demand on a composer, requiring that he create with the abandonment of an artist and the discipline of a precision mechanic. Dave composed to stop-watch and cue sheet, for his music must subtly acknowledge and change character on each of several "turns" within the length of a few bars and each cue be caught on a split-second timing. The splitting of seconds is literally true; musically, a single second is a vast time in which twenty-four frames of film will click through the projector and the orchestra can play a run of twenty-four fast notes or several loud full chords.

Dave set down his score in terms of a penciled "lead line," with indications of the harmonic and instrumental colors he had in mind. This was carried out into voiced and detailed orchestration by the arranger, whose work in turn was broken down into the separate instrumental parts by the copyists.

Since existing music seldom exactly suits a particular dramatic situation, film composers may derive, but they practically never steal. I'll admit to plenty of room for criticism in our use of music for the screen. We still, for example, suffer from the cliché—the stock fire music, the standard chase backgrounds, the obvious scoring under love scenes, the too pat catching of visual cues, and the shock cymbal crash as the camera finishes its tilt down to the calendar which reads "December 7." But more and more, the men of big talent are moving away from this, and producers are permitting it. Today, most film scoring is truly original composition. Much of it is very creditable. Occasional passages emerge from background scoring into mass recognition (Dave Raksin's "Laura" came from his score for that picture.) And some film scoring is recognized as having permanent musical value. Most of the composers I know are men of great integrity and enthusiasm as well as talent, and since film scoring offers more opportunity for experimentation than any other contemporary musical medium, they may well have an influence on the music of the future.

At nine o'clock in the morning of March 21st—just thirteen days after the close of photography—the orchestra members checked in through the studio gates from the parking lot across the street and began gathering in the big recording stage. This stage, too, is set up like a radio studio, but it is much larger and cluttered with a forest of microphone booms, music stands, choir platforms, and movable baffles. Three or four of the "men" were feminine, at the harp and in the cello and fiddle sections, and all these musicians were of the elite both in competence and income. Scale pay for a three-hour film recording session is $40.00, and the studio's current contract with the AFM guarantees an annual income of $6,916 to fifty musicians for their film work alone.

The doors closed. The pleasant caterwauling of tune-up sounded through the stage, and mixer Mike McLaughlin walked in from his glassed booth to supervise final rearrangement of the multiple microphone setup. Vital, ebullient Johnny Green shook down into his shirtsleeves, laid out his score on the stand, set up his split-second timing clock on the roomy podium and tapped his baton on the lamp to begin the session.

The conductor, as you know, is a sort of musical "producer," in that he envisions what he wants as a blended end product and adjusts the work of the individual musicians and choirs until he gets it. Dave stayed out in the mixer's booth to help in the balancing and check on the as-recorded version which he would hear from the booth loudspeaker.

The work went with what a non-musician would consider impossible rapidity. Johnny or Dave changed a note here and there—"Oboes, drop the B on bar 4 and come in on the B-flat." Johnny brought up the interpretation of this group and that choir—"Brass, bar 13 with crescendo to the cutoff, please." They cut a trial disc. The leaders of the several choirs went into the booth to listen to a playback, and Johnny brought the interpretation a little farther toward his goal. "Bar 6, chimes, play me a B just above the A on the third quarter" . . . . "Brass, the in-between eighth notes aren't speaking, not articulating. . . ." I felt the need of building even higher the feeling of triumph and reverence in the end title, and Johnny added an overlay of single-note chimes, composing on the spot and calling out the notes.

The next rehearsal was good, and Johnny buzzed for the picture. The overhead stage lights dimmed out. The stand lights glowed like golden pools in the darkness as they lit the faces of their instrumentalists, and on the white screen behind them the picture began to flicker. The white cue line moved across the screen, and when it touched the right edge Johnny's baton went down to start the take. . . . his mind simultaneously listening to the sound track through his left earphone, listening to the orchestra through his uncovered right ear, following his score, checking the second hand on his stop-watch and watching the picture on the screen, and conducting to split-second cues with perfect balance and spiritual feeling.

The film of the recording session came back from the lab the next day. Then the selected takes were patched with lengths of silent leader into reels corresponding to the picture, and the Sound Department set *Next Voice* up on its schedule for the re-recording.

This re-recording process is more commonly called "dubbing." It means that the assorted sounds for the picture—the dialogue, the sound effects, and the music, now spread around on several separate tracks—are played simultaneously and newly recorded on a single combined track, which later will be printed down the side of the composite prints for projection in the theatres.

The dubbing room itself is a miniature theatre. Deep leather chairs for the cutters, effects men, and other interested parties line the rear walls under the projection windows. Pin-point spotlights cone down softly on the gunmetal control desk where the two mixers sit before the dials, their hands on the "pots" which control the volume of each separate sound track channel, their eyes looking intently ahead at the picture on the screen.

The sound of the several tracks emerges from the loud-speaker up front as the "mix" in which it is being recorded. Below the screen an illuminated footage counter clicks

along as the picture unreels. Penciled cue sheets notify
the mixers as to what sounds are on which track, and
state the exact footage point at which each sound comes in.

The first rehearsal of a set of new tracks produces a
weird and wonderful jumble of sound from which it
seems that nothing intelligible or convincing could possibly
result. But as the reel is rehearsed over and over, and the
various sounds are controlled to their lifelike balance, you
begin to see that the creative process of telling the story
still goes on long after the picture is "finished."

There is a good deal of discussion as to how the sounds
should be handled and balanced at certain touchy spots.
"People ought to hear that radio set before they see it,"
says Margaret Booth, "I want to be grabbed the moment
I come in that room. I want to know somebody is talking
on the radio and it's important—make it tinny, push it. . . ."
And, "Put some character on that beat-up old car whenever you can, it's almost a personality." Cutter Jack Dunning leans forward in his leather chair. "Let's meet the
automobile on the incoming A track with engine noise
on the B." . . "The school bell's running long, take it
out at 237. . . . Can you smother that dialogue a little
without losing it, maybe a little filter, so it sounds like he's
really inside the phone booth." . . . "Bring up the kid's
slide; it's a plot point." And, of course, on the climactic
miracle rain, which worked out right only after much
earnest experimentation: "Take two beats after the radio
stops before you start the rain, then sneak it in. . . . Now
build it a little. . . . Catch the thunder, see if you can
sharpen it. . . . Ride up the rain when Mary comes to
Joe—and after the kid runs in, ride it as high as you can
go without blowing the tubes."

Now, the last step before preview, the reels went over to the laboratory, where the new combined sound track would be developed and printed and checked. And the picture track would be dressed with the optical effects which had hitherto appeared on the screen as title cards saying DISSOLVE or FADE.

These "opticals," by the way, are the film's form of punctuation. The cutter is entitled to make an instantaneous cut from one shot to another only when no slightest time lapse is involved, as when a character walks out of one room and into the next or when Joe dials the factory phone and Mary picks up the receiver at home. If a moderate time lapse is involved, such as that between Joe driving away from his house and driving into the plant, we dissolve; that is, the end of the first scene and the beginning of the second are overlapped in the printing so that one blends into another. (Incidentally, when Wellman would instruct, "After you finish the last speech walk over toward the window to give me some dissolve footage," he meant that he wanted to ensure having his dialogue in the clear, the dissolve blurring the screen only on nondescript action.)[1] A long lapse of time or a significant stop-and-fresh-start in the story is conventionally signaled by a fade, wherein the film printer fades down the end of one scene until the screen goes momentarily black and then fades up the beginning of the new start into full light. You might say that a cut is a film comma, a dissolve is a period or paragraph, and a fade is a chapter break.

Having dutifully set down the conventional film punctuation, I would like to air a personal phobia against the use of fades. I think the fade is an out-dated device, and I prefer to use instead a lengthened dissolve. This is not esoteric hairsplitting. The "full stop" of a fade breaks the continuity of image, and in my opinion a sustained continuity of image is a vital key to really full utilization of the film medium. I think the fade is a hangover from the old days when film was borrowing its construction from the stage, when we used to build our film stories in chunks, like acts. But we have come to realize that pictures do not need "intermissions" as the theatre does, and nowadays the best pictures move steadily along an upward line, with unbroken continuity of image and thought from beginning to conclusion.

The lab finished its work. The reels of the *Next Voice* picture and track were packed in those battered octagonal galvanized film cans and the word came to me that we were ready for preview.

I took a deep breath, crossed my fingers, and phoned Barrett Kiesling and Bill Golden to come over to the office and we'd set things up.

23

"A sneak preview is just what the term implies. The work print of the new picture is slipped in with the regular bill of a standard theatre without advance notice. The object is to get an honest audience reaction. Sometimes we also get surprised.

I was particularly anxious to get some dependable mass-audience reaction on *The Next Voice*. We thought we had a good picture. But we were too soaked in the project by now to be truly objective. We knew too much about the story; if there were a hole in the logic of the screen version we would tend to fill it in subconsciously from knowledge to which the audience would not have access. We were beginning to see the trees rather than the forest, we might be splitting hairs about things the audience would ignore. And in the final analysis the only dependable judge of what the mass of people will like is a cross-section of the people themselves.

The total of a picture is really half on the screen and half in the mass-emotion response to it of the people out front; we can't really tell what we've got until we sit there and watch the two halves go together. On the basis of what we learn during the preview, we make changes in the picture, to come as close as we can to bringing those two halves together with a perfect fit.

All this went double for *Next Voice*, for no picture like this had ever been made before; we had no precedent

to go by, no existing yardstick to measure the public's
taste. The paying public for any movie includes a lot of
teen-agers, and the great bulk of the American audience
is between the ages of eighteen and thirty years. We know
pretty well how they will react to musicals and melo-
dramas and comedies and the "type" pictures, but what
would they think of a picture about ordinary home life,
pregnancy, and God? We had to know, and we had to
know the unbiased, uncolored truth.

With the several studios previewing all their feature
productions in and around Los Angeles, it is not easy to
find a theatre where we can depend on getting a really
fresh audience reaction. The regular audience of a house
which runs a lot of previews quickly turns "pro." Its
reactions are self-conscious and, consequently, useless to
us. Also, many people in the industry like to get an advance look at their own and the other fellow's product,
and they make the rounds of the previews.

An audience of this sort betrays itself with flurries of
applause and hep comments on the credit titles. When you
hear wise whispers such as, "I thought Mellor was with
Stevens at Paramount," you know that you're going to
waste your evening. After the running you will get the
standard foyer routine of the taut handshake, the reverent
stare, and the "Basil, you've done it again!" This may make
you feel very good at the moment, but is small comfort
later on when the picture lies down and dies with typical
audiences. Small comfort of a different kind comes from
the cynical old studio hand who was annoyed at the way
the preview went. He looks at you grimly, shakes his head
and says dourly, "Needs a lotta work, my boy." I prefer
to bypass all the inside comments and put my trust in the

comments of the people for whom we actually make the pictures.

Too often, we think our plans for a sneak have been kept beautifully secret only to make our way into the theatre through a crowd of attractive young couples who turn out to be our studio messenger girls and their boyfriends. I decided that the sneak of *The Next Voice* would really be kept secret. And at the cost of being a bit cloak-and-daggerish at times, we succeeded.

First we decided to take the picture a goodly distance from Los Angeles. We settled on the United Artists Theatre, out in Pomona. Not only could we expect a real cross-section of the American audience—townspeople, farmers and ranchers, plus a sophisticated element from the nearby colleges—but the house had not staged a preview in years. Of course, this latter advantage would cost us the expense of installing a "dummy head" in the projection booth to permit running picture and sound on their separate work-version strips of film. But I thought it worthwhile and told Bill Golden to set the deal with the theatre manager. The deal, by the way, is usually an even exchange with no transfer of money; we get a small block of seats and some special service from the theatre personnel and the theatre gets a free attraction.

The date was set for Friday, March 24th. We had peeled the attendance list down to the scant dozen men and women whose presence was absolutely essential, and at noon on Friday they got their first notice, a suggestion that they keep the evening open and be on their phones at four o'clock. Golden and Stanley Markham of the publicity staff drove out to Pomona early to check on the equipment and the physical arrangements, and to rehearse

the theatre staff in how properly to distribute the preview
opinion cards, how to impress the audience to fill them
out, and how to handle the placing of the audience (babies
to the balcony, and so on) so as to minimize distractions
during the running.

At four o'clock, a dozen phones rang in different parts of
the studio, and the people were told to rendezvous at three
different spots around the lot at five o'clock. A misty rain
was beginning to fall.

At five o'clock three of the long black limousines drove
up to the separate rendezvous points and picked up their
passengers. The rain was coming down hard now. The
drivers nosed their cars out the different gates in different
directions, and when they were under way one person in
each of the cars broke out the sealed orders, to head for
dinner at the St. Charles Grill in Pomona. The cars swung
around for their forty-mile run through the rain and darkness down the San Bernardino Valley.

We all reached the St. Charles at about the same time.
The technicians who had ridden out in the print car would
hurry through dinner to get to the theatre early, but the
rest of us gathered in a small rear dining room. There were
Bill and Dottie Wellman and my assistant Walter Reilly,
who had driven down with Mrs. Schary and me; and
Music's Johnny Green, his wife Bunny, Supervising Cutter
Margaret Booth, and writer Cap Palmer from the other
car. Johnny is a wonderful entertainer, the steaks were
good after the long ride, and I was doing just fine until
suddenly everything hit me at once.

All previews are tense, if you've had anything to do
with the picture, but there was so much more at stake
on this one. Any husband who has driven his wife to

the hospital to have a baby will recognize my emotional state of, "It's all a mistake—we never should have gotten into this, let's go home." There was a vague fear—would this picture become known as Schary's Folly, would it become one of the famous failures? Some of the fears were uncomfortably specific: "We've come to the wrong town. . . . We picked the wrong night; it's a Friday and the house will be full of youngsters. Maybe I've made all the wrong decisions all the way through the picture. . . . Maybe I've ruined Wellman. . . . I pulled him into this wrong gamble and if we flop he'll be so disappointed." I was afraid the audience might not respond, then frightened that they might laugh too much at the wrong places, that people might even honestly consider the story irreverent and walk out. . . . And then, with the rain suddenly beating at the window behind me, I saw an awful vision of the big theatre with almost nobody there but us. The steaks were probably very good.

At eight-fifteen we got back in the cars and started for the theatre. The lights were shining on the wet black streets, the gutters were swimming with rain water and the three theatres we passed enroute were playing great pictures, wonderful shows, which had probably corralled all the audience in town, and why hadn't we chosen a theatre up on the main street where people could get to it? We turned the corner and pulled up beside the lighted marquee. The canvas banner MAJOR STUDIO PREVIEW TO-NIGHT flapped dismally in the rain, and one lone man was standing at the box office.

We gathered in the lobby, trying to look cheerful and nonchalant. Golden reported that the film was on hand okay, chief projectionist Merle Chamberlain was up in the booth and both cutters were on hand to cover emergencies, and Doug Shearer was inside on the fader. I wiped the rain off my glasses and peered through the crack in the aisle doors. My nose caught the smell of wet wool, and then my eyes got accustomed to the darkness and I saw that we had a packed house. We crossed our fingers and went inside to the little patch of empty seats.

The picture now drawing to its close on the screen was *Nancy Goes to Rio*. It was loud, colorful, musical, funny. The music swirled into its climactic finish, and I was glad we had arranged to break the mood by drawing the stage curtains and bringing up the house lights between the features.

Then the house lights faded down. The curtains drew apart, and on the screen came the title card announcing that this was a preview and would the audience please fill in opinion cards after the running. The studio Lion roared; he gave way to the title card *The Next Voice You Hear*, and then that wonderful joyously reverent music swept up and under the titles and faded as we dissolved into the tranquil morning establishing shot of the Joe Smith home. The music dropped out, we dissolved to Joe squeezing his oranges at the sink and Mary slitting her box tops, and the case began to go to the jury.

For those first few moments which always seem like years the audience just sat there. A few rows down a man stood up and pushed his way out past the people and walked up the aisle. Murder filled twelve hearts, until we saw that a very little boy was pulling him by the hand. Now young Johnny slid into the scene and the three people began the breakfast business. The camera went close on Joe as he looked upward and just chewed—suddenly there was

a snicker, it built into a laugh, and when the camera cut
to the twin shot of Johnny looking upward and chewing
in the same dead-pan fashion, the laugh built into a roar and
I let out my breath for the first time since the start.
The laughs kept rolling beautifully for the next two or
three minutes, and they were the warm sympathetic laughs
of people identifying themselves with the doings on the
screen. Joe and Johnny did their fast backout into the
other car, Johnny went to school, Joe checked into the aircraft locker room and, after the dissolve, came home in
the afternoon to the despised pot roast. The laughs were
running very high now. Were they too high?

Maybe we had withheld the introduction of our serious
note too long and had led the audience to expect farce
comedy all the way.

The film clicked inexorably closer to the one short
shot which I had felt all along would be our make-or-break
point. It was the moment at the beginning of the scene in
Johnny's room where Joe says, "A funny thing happened
on the radio just now . . ." and told about hearing the
Voice that claimed to be God. If the audience thought
that was funny, we were dead. But if we made that one
transition, we were over the hump. The scene kept coming
closer.

Joe finished the dishes and started in toward the living
room. We cut to Mary helping Johnny with his home
work. We cut back to Joe settling down with his paper and
glass at the radio. We cut back to the full shot across Mary
and Johnny toward the bedroom door. And then the door
opened and Joe stood in it, and Mary said, "You're not
listening to the radio—what's wrong?"

I should have trusted Bill Wellman. He had held back

the disclosure just the right time, balanced the scene like a celluloid ball on a column of air, and when Joe told about the Voice saying, "This is God. I will be with you for the next few days," the proverbial drop of the proverbial pin would have echoed through that house. We were home. There would be spot fixes as we went along, plenty of them, but we were home.

And now we could get back to our proper business and concentrate on the job in hand.

We expect the actions and the reactions of the preview audience to give us certain specific information. Those reactions should expose holes in our story and any blurry points in our logic. An expected climax which misses fire shows us where our building has been wrong, an unwanted laugh puts the finger on items which audiences can misunderstand. On the pleasanter side, we find throwaway lines or casual situations getting welcome unexpected laughs. We make a note to perhaps build those up, and if necessary to move back any essential dialogue which the laugh blots out.

Of course, we look up at the screen during the running only often enough to keep in touch By now we know the film frame by frame, and our eyes keep roving around the personal cross-section of people we've picked out to spot their reactions. We make mental notes of the points where the audience begins to wriggle in its seats, of the scenes which outstay their welcome until the popcorn bags begin to rattle, of the laughs which are late or hold an uncertain note.

Back at the beginning of all this I mentioned that, to make a good movie, a story must first possess that mysterious life-giving sparkle called showmanship. Here at the preview, you see that quality in action. It seems to be that

combination of elements which makes a group of people
function as an audience, instead of functioning as 800
individuals who happen to be confined within these walls.
Only when the picture is right do those individuals fuse
together into that whole which really constitutes an audience. When the picture is running really "hot," the row
of heads along an aisle moves as a unit, the faces all wear
the same expression.

Incidentally, this is one reason why I never put too much
trust in any statistical method of sampling audiences. You're
really sampling individuals. When those heads in the theatre
are moving as individuals, the picture isn't working. That's
why I wish all the critics would view the pictures they're
to write about, not in solitary state in a private projection
room, but right out there with the audiences for whom they
are writing.

The Next Voice kept on unreeling to a response that
seemed wonderful to us. There was one awful moment
when the voices of Joe and Mary suddenly lagged behind
their lip movement and we feared that a whole ten-minute
reel might be out of sync, but they came back in step on
the next dissolve; it was just a single faulty cut. There was
an unwanted laugh on Joe's coming home drunk, for
audiences have been conditioned over the years to laugh
automatically at the sight of intoxication, tragic or no.
(This spot was cured later by a rearrangement of order
which Bill was quick to see: in the final version, we cut
almost immediately from Joe's entrance to the shocked face
of his son, and the boy's closeup expression smothers the
laugh.) There was a scattering of unwelcome laughs when
the climactic rain began, after God's voice had prophesied

the miracle. Partly they rose from the coincidence of the
actual downpour of rain outside the theatre, but also they
betrayed the familiar nervous note and we crossed them
off as the unavoidable "relief" laughs we're apt to get during very tense moments or just afterward.

The final dangerous moment was in the church. Wellman's camera roves the tense, awe-struck audience, the
radio announcer leads into the phrase, "The next voice
you hear . . ." and on the screen there comes a pause, a
long pause of utter silence. If a baby cried, or a teen-age
comic blurted out some volunteer dialogue, we just didn't
know how the audience would react. But everybody in
that entire theatre brought to that moment the same respect
we had brought to its making, and the silence was very
moving. In a few minutes Mary was wheeled out of the
hospital delivery room, made her unconscious response to
Joe's loving touch on her ear, and our characters moved
up the corridor and out of our story. The house lights faded
up, people began to stand, and Wellman and I realized
from our stiff muscles that we hadn't moved since the picture began.

Out in the lobby, tables had been set up and the well-
rehearsed ushers were persuading people to stop long enough
to jot their opinions and suggestions on the printed preview
cards. The cards are simple. You can check various grades
from "poor" to "outstanding" on *How would you rate
this picture?* and *How would you rate the performances
of the following?* You check yes or no on *Will you recommend this picture to your friends?* You check whether
you're male or female, and check the age group in which
you fall. On this particular picture we also asked you to fill
in your church affiliation (and supplied a space for "none").

The cards are so printed that they can be folded up and mailed to the studio without a stamp, but we're human enough to want to end the suspense as soon as possible by getting the cards filled out before people leave the theatre.

Over at one side of the lobby our small group was huddled in the usual post-mortem. This is no time to feel good; while your impression of the audience and your recollection of its spot reactions is still fresh in your mind, you dig into the changes the picture needs and the ways in which it can be made better. But here, there were few changes. The conventional *The End* seemed too jarring an awakening, abrupt, and I decided to replace it with a companion Biblical verse to the one which opens the picture: it would not only be more appropriate to the mood, but would provide a start-and-finish frame around he story. Bill thought that one or two points would be put over more sharply by substituting different takes. Maybe that period of silence in the church was a trifle too long; we'd pull out one or two of the cutaways. But beyond those we had nothing much but the usual minor trims for pace and smooth flow.

We went back to the St. Charles for a gathering with the town's civic and religious leaders. Barrett Kiesling had arranged for them to see the picture and meet with us later as a sort of test for a similar method of selling the picture in the general market later on. Their opinions were very pleasant to hear. Bill Golden and Stan Markham stayed down at the theatre "counting the ballots" and telephoning in the returns every few minutes until we climbed back into the cars and pulled out in the rain for Los Angeles.

It was a long ride without much conversation. As the car pulled up into the driveway at my home shortly after one A.M. the phone was ringing inside. It was Bill Golden with his last report for the night. Out of 279 opinion cards, the picture was rated from "Very Good" to "Outstanding" by 266. To the vital question, *Will you recommend this picture to your friends?* the vote was *Yes—248, No—3.* The detailed analysis which Mildred Kelly and her helpers were making up during the night would show that an amazing 200 of the people who took the trouble to sign cards were in those make-or-break age groups, twelve to thirty years old. I wanted to call up everybody who had worked on the picture then and there and tell them about it and thank them for what they'd done. I compromised by calling Wellman and thanking him. Then I thanked God.

The best news of all came when the analysis was delivered the next afternoon. We had gambled that audiences would accept a picture about decent people doing good things, had risked violating the axioms that message pictures drive people away from the theatres and religion is poison at the box office. In the space left open for comments, card after card asked, "Why don't you make more pictures like this?"

24

Now that the baby had found out it could walk, it seemed to grow up overnight.

The approval of the Pomona preview audience had been so unusually fervent that, paradoxically, it worried us a bit. A certain type of attraction enjoys great success in the smaller towns, but misses fire in the large cities. Did the *Next Voice* fall in that unfortunate group? While it was admittedly a very human and unpretentious picture and we didn't exactly expect it to break into the Radio City Music Hall, nevertheless we had gambled on striking a vein of human interest common to all people, whether country or city, poor or rich, farmer or broker. We had to find out more clearly where we stood.

Bill Golden set up another sneak preview. But this one we scheduled for the Bay Theatre in Pacific Palisades, nicely accessible to Los Angeles' most "sophisticated" audience. Although we went through all the motions of secrecy, somehow the word leaked out, and on the Thursday night of the preview I could tell from the familiar faces in the lobby that we were going to get the test we wanted.

When the lights faded down and the title came on the screen, the butterflies beat their wings just as hard as at Pomona. And for those same awful first moments, the audience just sat there. But as it turned out, the warm little details of everyday living were about the same in

large homes as in small ones, and the power of God had
no relation to one's income bracket or degree of worldly
experience.

The cutter made a few last trims. The Music Department recorded the expanded end-title scoring. The Sound
Department ran its final re-recording, and the time came
for another of those executive decisions.

The decision that a picture is ready to go out entails the
same anxious responsibility as the original, "We'll do it."
Is it really ready? Are there things you still haven't thought
of which would increase its appeal? As long as you keep
the picture in your own hands at the studio you can keep
on improving it, but once you ship it that's the way it's
going to be and you'll stand or fall on it. Actually, I suppose
the feeling is akin to that of sending your child out into
the world.

I ought to mention here that a producer who is really
intent on his picture will run it some forty or fifty times
during this finishing stage, testing it again and again and
again, over-all and in detail. This is another thing whose
importance I learned from David Selznick: *"Run your
film."* Loose editing on a picture is often a result of the
failure of the people connected with it to run it as often
as they should. Constant running and scrutiny leads to a
seemingly effortless smooth and easy editorial flow. If a
producer picks up just nine or ten little cuts or trims in
each of his runnings, he eventually has made three or four
hundred such minor changes, and his picture, good or bad
over-all, at least has a fluidity of image.

But there is a breaking point in every picture at which
further improvements will cost more in time and money
than they are worth. I ran the picture at home one final

evening, slept on it, and the next morning sent out the word
to "Print and ship "   ·

The lab began cutting the precious negative into the
final version, and here and there around the lot the files
began to close. With re-takes no longer to be protected,
the costume lines were broken up, and the sets were listed
for striking as soon as their stage space was needed. Accounting drew lines under its columns, bundled up its
stacks of tabulating cards, and closed out the picture from
"In Process" to "Inventory." Purchasing filed away its req-
uisitions for dinner pails, and went back to its everyday
routine of buying airplanes, chicken feathers, ants, and
"three tons paraffin for ice (clear color, to see boy under)."

The studio promotional departments were racing down
their last lap, but soon they would close out too. Publicity's
Jim Merrick had captioned all his stills, the gallery had shot
the posters and cover art of the stars, George Nichols was
well along on planting the national magazine features, and
Don McElwaine was wrapping up Kiesling's exploitation
campaign material for Wheelright to take to New York.
Les Petersen, modernistically listed in the studio directory
under "Radio Activity," had the go-ahead to make *Next
Voice* one of his twelve monthly promotional specials, and
was arranging plugs on 150 or more network radio shows.
Tall Frank Whitbeck, silver-haired slogan-coiner from way
back, and his aide Herman Hoffman were working up the
advertising "trailer" which, showing in the theatres a week
ahead of the booking, would be responsible for a good percentage of the ticket purchases. The trailer would not be
easy to make, for the picture lacked the conventional hooks
on which to hang the dynamic hurry-hurry smash copy of
the cinema tradition. But at least most of the boys thought

it was a good picture, and they wouldn't have to hunt for a hedge like that wonderfully noncommittal slogan which blessed a famous clinker: "See It with Someone You Love."

Like any parent, I wanted to make sure that my youngster would go out into the world with the best possible opportunity to make his living. The M-G-M studio is only one part of Loew's, Inc.; it makes the product which other divisions distribute and exhibit. The selling is managed from the New York headquarters of the company. And so I arranged to go back there early in May to contribute whatever I could to the sales planning, and, humanly enough, to try to pass on my own enthusiasm to the men who would have to go out into the field and sell the picture.

All through the shooting the company had a running gag that whenever some unidentified stranger stood around the stage looking intently at anything he was tabbed as a scout for Pete Smith. Pete, as you know, makes the very funny shorts with Dave O'Brien, and he sometimes stretches his budgets by moving in on sets which feature productions have paid for. The night before I left for New York I took a few minutes to walk over to Stage 18. Our sets were still there. The walls and windows and doors were just the same, but all the props were gone, the people had moved away. It gave me a very lonely feeling. As I turned to go out, the night construction crew trundled its carts in through the big open door and set up work lights in the Joe Smith house. I looked at the foreman's alteration blueprint; the picture was listed as *Fixin' Fool*. And the producer? The Smith named Pete.

There is an old joke in the industry about a mysterious railway mail clerk who hates movies, this being the only explanation of the claim that all pictures are sensational in Hollywood, but by the time they reach the sales force in New York something has happened to them. We would lack that alibi; cutter Jack Dunning had flown east with the precious can containing our first composite print of *Next Voice*. But as I stood outside the Loew's Bldg. main projection room at 1540 Broadway and watched the ninety-man jury file in for the crucial showing, I couldn't help but wonder if my enthusiasm had clouded my judgment.

I looked at their faces: keen, smart men, men of great experience in selling pictures, managing theatres, creating advertising and exploitation. They had seen many, many pictures in their time, and this picture which was so important to me was now just Production 1488 to them. Nothing I could say or do would make any difference; it was all up to the picture. In the next hour and twenty minutes these specialists, using standards widely different from those at Pomona and the Bay Theatre, would either have decided that this was a picture they could sell, or that it was a turkey to be played off on the second half of double bills.

And once again the lights faded down.

It was a very long hour and twenty minutes. At last the lights went up. There was that same awful silence. But as Mr. Schenck walked past he gripped my shoulder hard, and whispered, "It's wonderful." And when I got the courage to look around I saw that a difference of three thousand miles in geography and a million miles in sophistication or interests was no difference at all in the hearts of people. Our child had adopted ninety foster parents.

Now, all the creative exploitation thinking and sales planning which had gone on on both coasts in many parts of the far-flung organization was brought together in a series of meetings with Mr. Nicholas Schenck, President of the entire Loew's organization, and Howard Dietz, who heads all Loew's advertising and exploitation.

It was agreed that *Next Voice* was a picture on which "word-of-mouth" comment passed along from person to person would be particularly important. We were pretty sure by now that the picture would be its own best sales-. man, and that the word-of-mouth from people who had seen it would be favorable.

Therefore, it seemed that the heart of our promotion effort would probably be an attempt to arrange an advance showing in every community a few weeks before the theatre engagement; the community leaders would be invited to the showing and we would trust the picture itself to persuade them to spread the word. Another line of effort, tying into the prominent radio angle of the story, would be to enlist the sympathy (articulate, of course) of radio commentators. Mr. L. K. Sidney suggested that the local theatre manager be encouraged to step out on his own stage in person a few days before the engagement to tell his audiences honestly what he thought of the coming picture. And we decided to send Jim Whitmore and Nancy Davis on separate tours around the country to visit key cities and meet the press and local drama critics, make appearances on local radio stations, speak at the meetings of various groups, and generally let their wonderfully clean, attractive young personalities project the atmosphere of the picture.

The promotion plans were good. But with all due respect to the picture, what *The Next Voice* campaign still urgently needed was that certain something variously described as a gimmick, a nub, an angle or a lead—in effect, it needed some single strong focal item which would draw the whole campaign together, which would carry the flag out in front of the parade, something equivalent to the prestige conferred on a picture by a pre-release engagement at the Radio City Music Hall. But this was not what you think of as a Music Hall type of picture. It had no name stars, no glamour, no spectacle, no eye-filling mounting of a lavish budget, none of the standard "draws" which are considered necessary to fill the world's biggest theatre.

Our tentative plans called for opening the picture on Broadway late in the summer, probably at the Astor Theatre where *Battleground* had run for so many weeks. A herniated disc in my back which had put me horizontal before I left the Coast now refused to be ignored any longer and I went to the hotel to go to bed for the rest of my stay in New York.

Mr. Schenck came up to visit me the next day, and while we were visiting, the phone rang. It was sales manager Bill Rodgers and he said, "How do you feel? Can you handle some good news?"

I said, "If it's good news, give it to the General," and I handed the phone to Mr. Schenck.

Mr. Schenck listened. His face lit up. He said, "That's great," and he smiled down at me. He said, "That's fine— sure, of course—that's wonderful!" Then he hung up.

He reached down and gripped my shoulder, as he had over at 1540 Broadway, just in time to save me from dying of curiosity about the call. He smiled again, and said, "Your picture goes into the Music Hall. I'm very proud." We called up the Coast and gave the news to Mr. Mayer, who was as excited and pleased about it as we were. Then after a little while Mr. Schenck went away.

For a few minutes, I lay there looking up at the ceiling and thinking. Periodically, in this business, you ask yourself, "Why do you go through this, the interminable hours and the hard work, the bitter disappointments and the kicks that you don't deserve and the slams that you do, and all the rest of it, why do you go through it?" And here, right here, was the answer. You go through it so that once in a while you can feel like this.

You had a notion, and you worked on it and it came out the way you hoped and maybe, at least for this little while, you're helping to pull your share of the wagon.

Well, the youngster was grown up. And it would go out into the world with the finest start we could give it.

Gradually the exhilaration wore off and I felt drained out. It was that feeling of utter, exhausted relief that comes, I suppose, to the "Father of the Bride" after the wedding. I'm male, American, and well over twenty-one, but candidly I felt like having a nice quiet cry all by myself. Then suddenly I remembered something I should have taken care of earlier. I reached over for the phone, called Jack Dunning in Washington and asked him if he had got hold of the war film clips for my next one, *Go for Broke*. Pirosh would be well along with the script back on the Coast, and we ought to get going.

25

Jim Whitmore and Nancy Davis appear on the screen in *The Next Voice You Hear* for something less than an hour and a half. That brief appearance called for months of earnest work on the part of several hundred unseen men and women from more than two hundred arts, trades and professions.

These men and women are skilled, talented, and hard-working. They are also widely misunderstood.

A few months ago the *New York Times Magazine* let me sound off on the subject of a satire I want to do some-time about Hollywood. It will be called *Welcome Home*, and it is the story of a man who goes back to his home town for a visit after ten years in the film industry. He is a perfectly normal man, weighed down with the problems of paying his income tax and getting his youngster's allergy cured and all the other things everybody worries about. The satire concerns the preconceived notions of his old friends.

It deals with the people who think all the talk about the money he makes in Hollywood is nonsense, but who still want to know if he can finance them in a business. It deals with the people who believe he makes a ridiculous amount of money in Hollywood but still assume he will touch them for a loan. It deals with the mother who wants to get her child into this "terrible" show business; with the writer who looks with contempt at Hollywood but

wants to sell a story to pictures—with the newspaper reporter who has a feeling that all Hollywood people are
crazy, but how about a job as a press agent out there?

In other words, this satire of mine will be aimed, not at
Hollywood, but at the things that people believe about
Hollywood, because that, to me, is always much more
comic.

Now let's take a real look at this phenomenal place.
Hollywood is a community located in North America
which has produced, is presently producing, and will con-
tinue to produce, the best and most definitive motion pictures in the entire world. Hollywood is bounded on the
North by legend, on the East by rumor, on the West by
scandal and on the South by superstition. Somewhere within
these boundaries lies the actual Hollywood community so
many talk about and so few really know.

Hollywood consists roughly of some 25,000 workers.
This amount is perhaps 1% of the population of Los Angeles, but this 1% contributes to the Los Angeles Community Chest Drive over 12% of the money raised. This group
of workers produces three to four hundred motion pictures
every year. These workers include not only actors, writers,
directors, and producers, but electricians, craftsmen of all
kinds, painters, leather workers, carpenters, designers, and
a variety of many other trades. Eighty percent of them
voted in the last Congressional election, and 99.7% voted
either Republican or Democrat—which doesn't leave much
for the Communists.

In the main, these people range in age from thirty to
sixty. Over 80% of the workers are male. Over 70% have
been working in the picture business more than ten years.
They came to films from many fields of activity—from

the amusement world, manufacturing, professional fields, finance, insurance, real estate, government, business, construction, transportation and personal service. Seventy-nine percent are married and 70% are married to the same partner they started out with. This figure of some 29% of divorces in Hollywood compares quite favorably with the Census report on the general divorce rate in the U.S. in 1947, which was 40%. The children of these marriages attend, in the main, public schools. Seventy percent of the families furnished members to the Armed Forces. Sixty percent of these people attend religious services regularly. Eighty-five percent of them are equipped with high-school education, or better.

These people, like everybody else, play golf, swim, play tennis, hunt, fish and ride, and have other amusements. The majority of them live in smallish single family homes and they come from every single state in the nation. Their hobbies include, like those of everybody else in America, reading, photography, music, gardening, puttering around the home with the children, cards, sporting events, traveling, painting, sketching, boating, riding, flying, horse races and going to the movies. The industry in which these people work has some $150,000,000 invested in Hollywood. The annual payroll in Hollywood in 1948 was a little over $251,000,000.

That is the Hollywood that everyone talks about, but so few know. Maybe so few know because of their mixed feelings toward movies.

There is a curious ambivalence in attitudes toward the motion picture. A man can admire Clark Gable and wish he were like Clark Gable. At the same time he can hate Clark Gable because, one, he is not like Clark Gable; two, his wife or sweetheart knows he isn't like Clark Gable; three, he can't hit a man on the nose and knock him down with one blow like Clark Gable. A man may admire Lana Turner because he'd like to put his arm around her. At the same time he hates her because he can't put his arm around her.

Because of this ambivalence, we are attacked from every angle. We are accused of being a reactionary town, interested only in a buck—of being enormously extravagant—and of being Communist controlled. We are attacked for not using the screen to say something, and we are accused of being propagandists and of filling the screen with "messages." We are viewed as a town tortured by labor strife, and we are told that, of course, there is no labor problem in Hollywood because we have corrupted and suborned the labor leaders. We are called insular, cut off from and oblivious to the world, and we are regarded as a transient community which has never sunk any roots. We are belabored for our story trends and cycles, and we are asked, "Why don't you make more westerns, more pictures on anti-Semitism, or injustice to the Negro?" Why don't you make more pictures like this and that, and then—why do you make so many pictures on one theme?

To make matters worse, Hollywood has become so much a part of American folklore that it has acquired a persistent stereotype in the public mind. There are all sorts of similar stereotypes, all more or less pernicious. No Englishman is supposed to have a sense of humor. All Italians are cowards and smell of garlic. Jews are parsimonious men with heavy accents. Negroes are lazy and dishonest and must be treated with a stern benevolence that only a Southern gentleman understands. The Irish are drunkards.

The self-perpetuating quality of these stereotypes is a

consequence of what is called the expectancy error. Let a humorless Englishman, a cowardly Italian, a parsimonious Jew, a lazy Negro, or a drunken Irishman attract observation and he is remembered, while all the witty Englishmen, the brave Italians, the generous Jews, the industrious Negroes, and the sober Irishmen are forgotten. People see what they look for.

Unfortunately, newspaper editors and reporters are constantly guilty of the expectancy error, at least as far as Hollywood is concerned, and in other directions too, I think. A lot of editors, I suspect, still believe that every boy hates school and wants to take his shoes off and go fishing, and that the boy, incidentally, has red hair and freckles. And if an American Indian fails to say, "Ugh, ugh," the reporters who write about him feel he ought to have said it and may put it in the story, anyway. Sometimes, unfortunately, we do the same thing in pictures, but we are trying earnestly to break the habit.

Now, what does this expectancy error do to news of Hollywood? To begin with, let me admit that most of the things you read about Hollywood are true. There are intellectual, spiritual and moral iniquities in the film community. There is divorce, adultery, plagiarism, perversion, cowardice, arrogance, cruelty, atheism, irresponsibility, communism, fascism, avarice and extravagance among motion-picture folk. But we are not unique in any of these sins —and that is the point I am trying to make. In between the fall of Babylon and the founding of Hollywood, there was no dearth of sin.

Nevertheless, sin in Hollywood has a tremendous edge over sin anywhere else when it comes to newspaper space, and public thinking in general. And it is ludicrous to see how far the press will sometimes go to associate sin with Hollywood. If a girl who had a single job in 1927 as an atmosphere player in a silent film becomes involved in any crime of even the slightest sordidness, she is a "Hollywood Actress," and, no matter how much drudgery it may mean for photographic retouchers, she is "beautiful." The trouble is that people don't have this "expectancy" of sin in Detroit, and Seattle and Birmingham. They aren't watching for it, and anyway it doesn't have glamour. So they forget it and remember the sins of Hollywood.

But the stereotype involves more than sin. It involves our personal and industrial pursuits, and it was pretty well crystallized twenty-two years ago by the very amusing play *Once in a Lifetime*. How was it created in the beginning? It was partly superimposed, and partly generated from within.

To begin with, motion pictures share the smudged reputation that all the arts have inherited from the time when "manly" men were either warriors, statesmen, hunters or farmers, and decent women spun and wove and reproduced. And motion pictures also share the particular disreputability bequeathed to show business by the puritanism and rigor of the American frontier. And even within show business, motion pictures started out as a bastard form. The theatre folk—actors, playwrights, stage directors—had in the beginning a real contempt for the new medium. It was a cast-out among cast-outs. Financial reward, the inducement which ultimately lured the theatre people to the screen, was not available for a long time. Then, further, Hollywood has shared the reputation of another demi-monde, Southern California, with its orange trees and sunshine and religious cults—a new place, which was a small community when the film industry moved here. As the community and the industry grew, the show folk and the vacationers and the seekers for a new life exchanged influences as well as reputations.

And as I said, we generated a goodly part of our own reputation (along with Southern California's) from within. The publicity department of the industry developed white Rolls-Royces, spoke of half-dressed women, prepared gag shots of people reading newspapers and eating lunch in swimming pools. They were selling glamour, and they created a folk tale in which empty-headed vulgar men and men with thick accents sat in enormous, over-decorated offices and squandered fortunes on their whims, while forgotten writers, drawing great salaries, made adolescent passes at blonde secretaries, and sometimes got bricked up in their cubicles and lost forever during reconstruction projects. At night, of course, everyone went home to houses full of bear rugs littered with unclad women.

As a producer—one of the major figures in this stereotype—I can report, with only a tiny twinge of regret, that I never had any of these advantages. The stories made good telling, I suppose, back on Broadway, but whatever factual basis they may have had, two decades ago when the whole country was in a more extravagant phase, is long gone. And yet we are still guilty of perpetuating the legend from within. I know that I have sometimes told Hollywood jokes which have only encouraged the stereotype that I am deploring.

Eighteen years ago, when I came to Hollywood as a writer, there was a writer's costume, a sort of uniform. gray-flannel trousers, dark-brown jacket, sport shirt and a colored scarf, and thick, rubber-soled shoes. Sure, I wore it myself. It was part of the "release" of coming out from New York. Hollywood was a far place, a place for fun and comfort and relaxation—not for real creative effort.

Now that's changed. Writers wear suits and shirts and ties, and they comb their hair, and their shoes are either black or brown, not two-toned. But the change is more fundamental than an altered costume. The basic change is in the writer's attitude toward his work. Once he came out here only to make money, so he could go back and write a play or a great American novel. Now he knows that the motion picture is a medium in itself from which he can derive great satisfaction. His early frustrations arose from his inability to control his work, from the sometimes ruthless misuse of his work, from the multiple credit system. You never see nowadays what you used to see, what used to be a joke . . . original story by—based on an idea by—adaptation by—screenplay by—additional dialogue by—comedy construction by—up to fifteen names. Now, essentially, you see the name of one writer or a team of writers. Producers have become careful in their selections and writers are participating more fully in their projects, seeing them through. The writer's status has improved further with the emergence of the writer-director and the writer-producer.

As for the stereotyped conception that we are wasteful, fumbling, extravagant, it just is not true. The most irritating question I know is. "Why do you make so many bad pictures?" It shows absolutely no understanding of any art form. Every art has a greater percentage of failure than success. That isn't unique to Hollywood. It's true of the theatre, of novels, of magazine writing, of newspapers, sculpture, painting, everything. It's inevitable. But when you consider the tremendous pressures put on us, the time tables, the time-clocks that we work under, the demand for product in quantity, I think we do extraordinarily well. I'll compare our facts and figures, in terms of artistic or financial success or failure with the theatre, which, by comparison, is a free and uninhibited art. We do have successes; you'll remember many you've enjoyed.

Once, on a train, a man asked me what business I was in. Reluctantly, I told him, and he asked the inevitable question: "How do you make so many bad pictures?" It turned out he was a manufacturer of neckties. So I smiled and said, "Take a look around this club car." He looked, and he didn't ask any more about pictures.

One thing that must be remembered is that we are irrevocably committed to our mistakes by the economics of our business. When we have a disaster, everybody knows about it. In automobile engineering there have been horrible errors—whole die blocks or assembly lines have had to be remade. But those errors were hidden, not broadcast to the public as hot news. Leo Rosten's economic study of film making proved that our percentage of error is no greater than that in any other industry.

There was a period, in the early days of talking pictures, when stories were purchased with such desperate haste that six out of ten properties bought were never made. The average was 60% abandonment. I have convinced myself that it is possible to operate on a 20% abandonment and, during the last year and a half at our own plant, we have operated on an even smaller margin. We have been careful. We haven't worried about losing a story property to a competitor, and we haven't bought a story unless there was need for it in terms of immediate production plans.

There are two more things which the industry must consider about the stereotype of Hollywood. Does it do us any harm? And, if so, how can we combat it?

Aside from my personal distaste for being the subject of an exaggerated and dated stereotype, and of having it directed at my children and my community, I think it hurts the motion-picture community economically. There are those within the industry who disagree with me. They say that the stereotype is glamour, that the reputation for sin is salable at the box-office, that the facts about our industrial operations should be hidden behind a veil of mystery, and that the misconceptions about our extravagance and waste should be encouraged lest people lose their belief in Hollywood's magnificence. They say: "Thank God the newspapers give a Hollywood scandal unjustified attention. If they didn't we'd be slipping."

This thinking, I say, is antiquated. It is all a part of saying: "Don't release stills showing that a marble palace is made of canvas and plaster. Don't let the public know what a process shot is. Don't let them know that So-and-so is married and has two children." That doesn't make sense, and I can prove it. Every year I wrestle with film on some forty or more pictures. I know the scripts, I've worked on the casting, I've looked at the rushes and production tests, I've spent time on the sets. And yet, when I go to a preview, despite all my information about the picture, I still respond to it as a member of an audience. And so does everybody else who makes pictures.

The stereotype handicaps the film industry in discharging its commitment to be all things to all men. We have not yet been able to evolve, because of our economic set-up, a specialized picture for a specialized, hence small,

audience. In a sense this policy of making all pictures for
the universal audience may be a handicap—it is certainly a
responsibility. A picture of major-studio quality cannot be
made, nowadays, for much less than $500,000. That pic-
ture may not break even until the public buys more than
$2,000,000 worth of tickets to see it. Obviously, it re-
quires a mass audience.

Now, whenever any group of people begins to develop
a rigid attitude toward Hollywood, a false conception
about what pictures contain and how they are made, those
people will stay away from the box-office. Some will be
morally offended by their image of Hollywood; others
will be intellectually offended. If a segment of the potential
audience becomes convinced that Hollywood makes nothing but musicals, we will lose some of that segment. We'll
lose a segment which comes to believe that Hollywood
has not broadened its intellectual horizon in twenty years,
or that Hollywood makes nothing but message pictures, or
that Hollywood has ignored its social responsibilities, or
that Hollywood is peopled with degenerate men and scar-
let women.

As for the stereotype as a newspaper space-getter, I
think I can show that that kind of publicity doesn't mean
anything at the box-office. Because of a specific stereotype
which grew up around her, Miss Greta Garbo attracted
more newspaper attention than any other actress between
1925 and 1940. And yet Miss Garbo's films were never
great financial successes in the United States—her largest
audience was abroad, and many of her pictures barely re-
couped their negative cost in the domestic market. After a
tremendous avalanche of publicity had attended Douglas
Corrigan's "wrong-way" flight to Ireland, RKO signed

him for a picture The picture was a failure. Famous ath-
letes have never lived up to expectations at the box-office
when they appeared on the screen. In short, newspaper attention which does not directly concern the work of an
actor in motion pictures is no help at the ticket window,
will even be harmful if it destroys the public belief in the
integrity of an actor's work. An actress who is seen on the
screen as a siren and a temptress cannot hurt herself by
scandalous behavior in public. But if the actress plays nuns
or saints, she can limit her effectiveness by gaining a flam-
boyant public reputation.

Now what can we do about the stereotype? Well, for
instance, in our advertising, we are learning not to subor-
dinate everything to cheesecake. We have stopped selling
pictures like *Mrs. Miniver* or *The Best Years of Our Lives*
on the basis of "What was Tillie doing last night?" or "She
was a woman all men wanted." And while we are still
guilty of some misuse of advertising, we are not unique
in that respect. The use of superlatives in advertising is inherent in the American scene; pick up any magazine and
you'll find the razor your face doesn't feel or the tooth-
paste that will make women pursue you. We're far from
perfect. But we're trying.

We can and should extend our present efforts in the direction of public education about the industry, its product
and its people. We should have more personal appearances
by stars and other personalities who can speak articulately
about their industry.

Recently at our own studio we have started opposing
the stereotype from another angle. We are instituting a
series of lectures for our new players warning them against
cliché publicity and tawdry publicity, explaining to them

that their careers do not depend on flashy automobiles and night-club exploits. We are saying to them, "If you want to get married, try to keep from dashing off somewhere in the middle of the night to do it." We are going to ask them to make their public conduct a little more dignified, a little more reserved, a little more fitting to their position in the public eye.

Finally, there is nothing we can do about marital tangles and obstetrical irregularities, if they occur, except to keep on disseminating genuine information about the great majority of our people who live in dignity and decency, and reducing the amount of nonsense in our press releases, so that the public will view our scandals in their proper frame of reference, the same frame of reference which exists in Milwaukee and Paducah.

The most hopeful thing is that motion pictures, themselves, are improving. They are, I think, to a great extent a reflection of American education and culture. We know, for instance, that twenty years ago the average education of our audience was a trifle below that of a grammar-school graduate. Now it has reached the second year of high school. It is reasonable to suppose that, in another twenty years, it will have reached the high-school graduation level. Man's life and leisure are expanding, so he has more time for education.

And as the intellectual level of our audience improves, the demands on us increase—which means that our pictures must get better and better. We must abandon cheap tricks of dramaturgy and conceive our pictures better. We are already doing so. It is no accident that some films are discussing vital questions like anti-Semitism, injustice to Negroes, sex education. We are motivated neither by altruistic desire to inform the public nor by venal desire to exploit it. We are simply trying to give the public what it wants. Motion pictures have always been at one with American society, reflecting what is going on in America. We have never been much ahead of or much behind our audience at any time. We have given the audience what it wants, and now, I think, it wants more thought-provoking pictures.

I don't say that Hollywood is a typical American community, because that would be dishonest. But our characteristics, as a show business, are typically American. We are what the people expect us to be and what they insist on criticizing. As individuals we are probably more emotional, expressive, extroverted, than the norm. That is the nature of show business. But I know that the men around me are stable, normal folk who work their brains out.

My friends do not keep strings of women and little black books full of juicy telephone numbers, as visitors to Hollywood usually hope they do. My friends get up early, go to bed at a respectable hour; and they can't get drunk any more than a grocer can in Kansas City, because they have to work hard the next day, too. They spend their vacations with their families, and they are concerned about where their youngsters go to school. They indulge in a normal amount of seduction and divorce, and marriage and church-going, and gambling and charity-giving.

But despite the fact that whatever they do is exaggerated, by virtue of their position as the entertainers of America, they are a credit to the American social scene. I think they have made an enormous contribution to their fellow men in terms of entertainment—and, more important, in terms of elevation of the human spirit.

These are the people who made *The Next Voice You*

Hear. This has been their story. By now, you know them. And if you have begun to share some of my sincere respect and deep affection for them, and for what they do, I am very glad indeed we ran into each other all those pages ago outside that preview at the Bay.

Crew, Credits and Cast of

The Next Voice You Hear

PRODUCER	Dore Schary
DIRECTOR	William A. Wellman
SCREEN WRITER	Charles Schnee
STORY BASIS	George Sumner Albee
MUSIC BY	David Raksin
ART DIRECTORS	Cedric Gibbons and Eddie Imazu

PRODUCTION CREW
UNIT MANAGER	Ruby Rosenberg
ASSISTANT DIRECTOR	Joel Freeman
2ND ASSISTANT	Fletcher Clark
SCRIPT SUPERVISOR	Bill Hole

CASTING DIRECTOR, ASSOCIATE	Leonard Murphy
ASSISTANT	James Broderick

FILM EDITOR	John Dunning
ASSISTANT CUTTER	Greydon Gilmer

CAMERA CREW
DIRECTOR OF PHOTOGRAPHY	William Mellor
OPERATOR	Neal Beckner
ASSISTANT	Matt Kluznick
2ND ASSISTANT	King Baggot, Jr.
STILL MAN	Eddie Hubbell

RECORDING SUPERVISOR	Douglas Shearer
SOUND MIXER	Conrad Kahn
SOUND STAGE MAN	Fred Faust
SOUND 2ND MAN	Bill Edmonson

SET DECORATIONS	Edwin B. Willis
ASSOCIATE	Ralph S. Hurst
ASSISTANT	William Skamnes

PROP MAN	James Luttrell
ASSISTANT	Dick Hendrickson
WARDROBE MAN	Bob Streeter
WARDROBE LADY	Florance Hackett
ELECTRICAL CREW	
GAFFER	Chester Philbrick
BEST BOY	Howard Roberts
CREWMEN	Eugene W. Stout
	Frank Huszar
	Zeb Bojarsky
	William McConnell
	J. Toney
	Lee Cannon
GRIP DEPARTMENT	
HEAD GRIP	Leo Monlon
2ND GRIP	Les Coleman
CREWMEN	Don Larson
	Art Spang
REAR-PROJ. PROCESS STAGE	
DIRECTOR OF PHOTOGRAPHY	Hal Marzorati
PROCESS ASSISTANT	Dan Powers
PROCESS ASSISTANT	Carroll Shepphird
GRIP	Joe Gabourie
SECOND UNIT	
DIRECTOR	John Waters
DIRECTOR OF PHOTOGRAPHY	Harold Lipstein
DIRECTOR OF PHOTOGRAPHY	Max Fabian (Process)
SECOND CAMERAMAN	John Nickolaus
ASSISTANT CAMERAMAN	A. C. Riley
ASSISTANT DIRECTOR	Bert Spurlin
GAFFER	Bill Allen
BEST BOY	George Lasher
SCRIPT SUPERVISOR	William Orr
GRIP	Harold Constable
GRIP	Roy Strickland

STANDBY PAINTER	Frank Wesselhoff
LABORER	Al Simpson
LOCATIONS	Howard Horton
	Charles Coleman
PUBLICITY UNIT MAN	James W. Merrick
STAND-INS	Jack Harris
	Phoebe Campbell
	Dorothy Whalen
	Henry Stone
	Billy Cartledge
	Venita Murdock
	Ike Isaacs
	Ben Watson
	Bill Scully
	Dick Ames
STUNT DOUBLES	Jack Semple
	Harry Wollman

Together with the several hundred men and women of the studio whose contributions to the picture, often sufficiently direct to be mentioned in the book, were made off the stages.

The Featured Cast

James Whitmore   Nancy Davis

Gary Gray   Lillian Bronson
Art Smith   Tom d'Andrea
Jeff Corey   Douglas Kennedy

George Chandler

Together with the many feature, bit, extra, and atmosphere players whose appearance and skill contributed greatly to the interest and validity of the picture.